or more than 25 years, The Institute of Internal Auditors has looked to The Research Foundation to define leading internal audit practices and to promote the profession to academic institutions. The Foundation's board of trustees recently redefined their mission as:

> *"To be the recognized leader in sponsoring and disseminating research, to assist and guide internal auditing professionals and others, in the areas of risk management, controls, governance processes and audit practices."*

The Research Foundation is committed to:
- Defining internal auditing practices as performed by global leaders in research reports.
- Educating practitioners, educators, and the general public about the merits of internal auditing.
- Distributing materials on the benefits of internal auditing to organizational leaders and clients.

To continue to benefit from this ongoing effort and to help The Foundation fund top-quality research studies and educational programs for internal auditors worldwide, join the Master Key Program. For $1,000, your organization can become a subscriber and receive all Research Foundation publications and research reports as soon as they come off the press.

2001 Master Key subscribers will receive titles like:
- *An e-Risk Primer*
- *Independence and Objectivity: A Framework for Internal Auditors*
- *Internal Auditing Reengineering: Survey, Model, and Best Practices*
- *Enterprise Risk Management: Trends and Emerging Practices*
- *Effective Compliance Systems*
- *Fraud and Its Deterrence*
- *Value Added Services of Internal Auditors*

To subscribe to the Master Key Program, call: +1-407-830-7600, Ext. 279 or e-mail: research@theiia.org

Count on The IIA Research Foundation to help you perfect your profession and empower your success. Subscribe today.

To order individual copies of Research Foundation reports:
Online: www.theiia.org under The IIA
E-mail: iiapubs@pbd.org

EFFECTIVE COMPLIANCE SYSTEMS:
A PRACTICAL GUIDE FOR EDUCATIONAL INSTITUTIONS

By
David B. Crawford, CIA, CCSA, CPA,
Charles G. Chaffin, CIA, CPA,
and Scott Scarborough, CIA, CISA, CPA

The Institute of Internal Auditors Research Foundation

The Professional Practices Framework for Internal Auditing (PPF) was designed by The IIA Board of Directors' Guidance Task Force to appropriately organize the full range of existing and developing practice guidance for the profession. Based on the definition of internal auditing, the PPF comprises *Ethics* and *Standards, Practice Advisories,* and *Development and Practice Aids,* and paves the way to world-class internal auditing.

This guidance fits into the Framework under the heading *Development and Practice Aids.*

ISBN 0-89413-467-1
01337   11/01
First Printing

The conference and this book are dedicated
to
Allen O. Hinkle

Allen O. Hinkle was born August 22, 1919, in Lockhart, Texas. He received his BBA degree from The University of Texas in 1941. He also attended Northwestern University and Harvard University. Mr. Hinkle completed the management course at The University of Pittsburgh in 1958. He was a member of Beta Alpha Psi National Honor Accounting Fraternity. He served with the U.S. Navy as a supply officer during World War II.

Allen began his career with Humble Oil and Refining Company, which later become Exxon and then ExxonMobil Corporation. He held numerous assignments with Humble and Exxon, including the positions of Assistant Controller and General Auditor of Exxon Company U.S.A. He held memberships in The Institute of Internal Auditors, the American Society of Certified Public Accountants, the Texas Society of Certified Public Accountants, the American Petroleum Institute, and the Financial Executives Institute.

He received the Thurston Award in 1962 from The Institute of Internal Auditors, and in 1969, he was a recipient of the Distinguished Alumni Award of The University of Texas at Austin College of Business Administration (now the McCombs School of Business).

Among his many accomplishments, Mr. Hinkle was instrumental in developing the Exxon Standards of Business Conduct, including the Conflict of Interest and Ethics policies. He was also a leader in developing the Basic Standards of Management Controls to provide management with the basic criteria for cost effective control processes. These policies and procedures continue to be key elements of ExxonMobil's operating practices. He can also be credited with promoting similar practices and procedures throughout industry.

Mr. Hinkle's efforts in the area of ethics, code of conduct, and management controls in business helped to lay the foundations for today's effective compliance and risk management systems. The Institute of Internal Auditors and the authors are proud to dedicate this work to such a pioneer as Allen O. Hinkle.

CONTENTS

The Institute of Internal Auditors Research Foundation

Appendices

TABLES AND FIGURES

Tables

Figures

The Institute of Internal Auditors Research Foundation

ABOUT THE AUTHORS

David B. Crawford, CIA, CCSA, CPA, is the principal author. He is an Audit Manager Emeritus in The University of Texas System Audit Office with responsibilities in the system-wide institutional compliance program in which he has been intimately involved for three years.

He held previous audit management positions with The University of Texas System Audit Office, The State Auditor's Office of Texas, the City of Long Beach Auditor's Office, and Texas Southern University Audit Office in Houston, Texas. In addition, he held senior financial, information, and production management positions in several large commercial firms and various agencies in both city and state governments.

Crawford currently provides training and consulting services worldwide as a principal in JDEnterprises, a company he owns with his wife, Justina. Areas of concentration include risk management, risk-based auditing, internal controls, COSO, risk and control self-assessment, and managing the internal audit department. He is frequently a speaker at professional auditing conferences in North America, Europe, and Africa. Recently, he authored an article in *Internal Auditor* on the Levels of Control in the COSO Model.

Charles G. Chaffin, CIA, CPA, is a collaborating author. He is the Director of Audits for The University of Texas System with overall responsibility for all internal auditing activities in the system. He is also the System-wide Compliance Officer responsible for providing guidance to the various component compliance programs and information to the system's executive management and board of regents. He has been, since its inception in January 1998, the U.T. System official primarily responsible for the development and implementation of the U.T. System Institutional Compliance Program. He previously was an audit partner in Deloitte and Touche in Houston, Texas.

Chaffin is a frequent presenter at professional auditing and compliance conferences. He is currently regarded as one of the most knowledgeable practitioners in compliance in higher education.

The Institute of Internal Auditors Research Foundation

Scott Scarborough, CIA, CISA, CPA, is a collaborating author. He is the Vice President for Business Affairs and the Compliance Officer at The University of Texas at Tyler where his responsibilities include financial services, human resources, physical plant, environmental health and safety, information resources, university police, a performing arts center, and institutional compliance. He previously held the position of audit manager at The University of Texas System Audit Office and was also an audit supervisor with PriceWaterhouseCoopers.

Scarborough authored the first *Action Plan to Ensure Institutional Compliance* for the U.T. System. In addition, he prepared the original draft of the Standards of Conduct Guide shown as Appendix H. He was the initiator of control self-assessment in the U.T. System and presented at many internal auditing conferences on this subject. Scarborough is currently a doctoral student in strategic management at The University of Texas at Arlington.

ACKNOWLEDGMENTS

Special thanks and appreciation to:

- The Institute of Internal Auditors Research Foundation for their support and advice.

- Dr. Urton Anderson of The University of Texas at Austin for his encouragement and review as the writing progressed.

- The University of Texas System Institutional Compliance Program for permission to use its documents and experiences.

- Stanford University for permission to include its institutional compliance plan.

- Justina A. Crawford for performing all of the editing duties and ensuring that the information is presented in a way that would make sense to all members of the higher education community, not just compliance and internal auditing personnel.

EXECUTIVE SUMMARY

Background

When The University of Texas System embarked upon their institutional compliance initiative in January 1998, they found a complete absence of information and experience in the design and application of a comprehensive institutional compliance program for institutions of higher education. The only existing body of knowledge available dealt exclusively with the health-related activities of institutions of higher education, specifically with teaching hospitals. As The University of Texas System endeavored to establish an institutional compliance program that covered all activities within the system, it was faced with adapting practices from the health field, using trial and error to establish best practices in uncharted areas, and developing a new body of knowledge applicable to the academic side of higher education. This book is that new body of knowledge.

Because of the unique structure of the U.T. System — 16 virtually autonomous institutions under a single board of regents — the knowledge gained in the three years that this program has been operational is applicable to all of higher education. The 16 components range in size from less than 5,000 students to over 50,000. Of the 16, nine are academic institutions, six are health related, and one is the central administration unit that provides common services to the other 15 institutions or components, as they are known within the system. The nine academic components include a comprehensive flagship institution with significant graduate programs, research and a major intercollegiate athletic program, several mid-size institutions that have some graduate programs and associated research, and several small institutions whose primary focus is on undergraduate instruction. The six health-related components include one of the world's leading cancer hospital and research centers, two other hospitals, and numerous medical related schools. Consequently, virtually any institution of higher education can find a component within the U.T. System to which it is similar.

During the preparation for the Effective Compliance Systems Conference it was discovered that three years after the U.T. System had begun its journey into compliance, there still was no other comprehensive institutional compliance program operational in higher education. The conference and this book are intended to share the information learned in the U.T. System experience with others who are finding it increasingly necessary to implement an institutional compliance program. This is a "how to" book intended to take you step by step through the implementation of a comprehensive institutional compliance program at your institution.

The Institute of Internal Auditors Research Foundation

Why and What

The Introduction and Chapters 1 and 2 provide information on why this book is being written, why your institution needs an effective compliance program, and what are the required components of such a program. They are the foundation upon which all else is built. The book is necessary because of a lack of information on non-health-related compliance programs in educational institutions. Your institution needs an effective compliance program to avoid monetary loss, damage to reputation, and demands on executive management time. The compliance program you need should follow the requirements established by the *U.S. Sentencing Guidelines for Organizations*. These three sections should convince you that you need to implement an effective compliance program. Once you reach that decision, all you need to know is how to accomplish that task successfully. Chapters 3 through 12 provide you with a road map for that journey.

How To

The steps for implementing an effective compliance program are summarized in Appendix G and presented in detail in Chapters 3 through 12. Each chapter deals with a major segment of steps in the process. Detailed information on accomplishing each step is presented and important lessons learned are highlighted.

Starting

How you start (Chapter 3) your implementation effort will have a major impact upon its success. There are six key lessons learned in this area that will aid in your implementation:

- Obtain outside help to begin an effective compliance program.
- Include representatives from all facets of the institutional community (faculty, staff, administrators, students, etc.) on the committee charged with designing the compliance program.
- Make compliance personally relevant to each individual employee.
- Choose your words for describing the compliance program carefully.
- Obtain a Board of Regent's resolution establishing the program and its objectives to give it authority and emphasis.
- Set a realistic implementation timeframe; you may expect implementation to take up to five years.

A Champion

The keystone of an effective compliance program is the chief executive officer (Chapter 4). This person is the compliance program champion. To be that champion, the chief executive officer (CEO) must understand the positive impact that an effective compliance program can have upon the overall management process of the institution. In addition, the CEO must lead by example and be a visible presence in the program. This presence may be physical, such as attendance at compliance meetings and functions; or it may be demonstrated by the appropriate allocation of institutional time and financial resources to the compliance program. Finally, the chief executive officer must understand that an effective compliance program requires open communication and trust within the institution.

Building an Infrastructure

During the first six months of implementation (Chapter 5) the chief executive officer must establish the infrastructure, which will be the backbone of the compliance program. The compliance officer, the compliance committee, and the compliance committee working group must all be appointed. In addition, a decision must be made regarding the appropriate organization of the compliance function. Once again, how each of these tasks is carried out can have significant ramifications on the success of the program. Experience indicates the following:

- Start with what you have and build on it; don't wait until everything is perfect.
- Consider carefully all the advantages and *disadvantages* before appointing a current member of executive management as the compliance officer.
- Choose someone with previous assurance experience, such as an internal auditor, to be in charge of the day-to-day activities of the compliance function.
- Provide training for all players in the compliance infrastructure, even if you have to hire outsiders to do it, and capture that training so that as new players come on board they can be properly trained.

Advertising the Compliance Program

Once the infrastructure is in place, the compliance officer and compliance committee face the task of informing all employees about the compliance program. To accomplish this, a standards of conduct guide that is applicable to the majority of employees should be developed and from it a generalized compliance training program must be established. This task seems simple but it took the U.T. System over three years to accomplish it. Lessons learned include:

- Do not establish new policy with the standards of conduct guide; it should be an abstract of current policies applicable to most employees stated in understandable language.
- Once again, include all segments of the institutional community in the development of this guide.
- Review, review, review is the watchword for the guide and the training program developed from it; including legal review, content review, and presentation review.
- Choose a combination of delivery training mechanisms for general compliance training that works for your institution.
- Design a common testing mechanism that can be used with all delivery methods

Which Compliance Risks are Significant to the Institution?

Determination of those compliance risks that can have critical impact upon the institution involves everyone in the institution (Chapter 7). The risk assessment process is detailed, but easy to follow. There are, however, several lessons learned that can save you false starts and unexpected compliance exposures, namely:

- Use a bottom-up risk assessment methodology.
- Never exclude a risk just because it has not happened at your institution or because you think it will not happen.
- Consider every risk as if there were no current mitigation strategies in place; that is, do not exclude a risk because you think it is already well managed.
- If the list of risks that can have critical impact on your institution seems insurmountable, stratify the list into (a) those for immediate attention, (b) those you believe are already well managed, and (c) those that can be addressed later.
- Do Not Get Complacent. Risk assessment is continuous; risk can change at any time and something you have not even identified today can be your most critical risk tomorrow.

How to Manage the Critical Risks?

Managing the critical risks is the "guts" of an effective compliance program (Chapter 8). There are four components to managing the critical risks; (1) a responsible party, (2) a monitoring plan, (3) a specialized training plan, and (4) a reporting plan. We have even suggested in Chapter 10 that there should be a fifth component, a consequence of a noncompliance plan; however, that is just a suggestion. (Read Chapter 10 to see why.) Some of the lessons learned which will help you to properly manage your critical risks are:

- There can be only one (1) responsible party for a risk. If it seems like there are two or more responsible parties, you probably have two or more risks.

The Institute of Internal Auditors Research Foundation

- The responsible party should seek the help of an assurance professional (from the compliance function or internal auditing) to develop the monitoring plan for the risk.
- Only knowing that there are instances of noncompliance is useless. Knowing why they occurred is power; the power to minimize reoccurrence.

Assurance Strategies

Monitoring and auditing for noncompliance are requirements of an effective compliance program. The U.T. System developed a range of assurance strategies, which are presented in Table 11 and include certifications, inspections, agreed upon procedures, audits, peer reviews, and external assurance providers. Several lessons learned involving assurance strategies are:

- Certification should be used for all operational units, even when other assurance strategies are to be used on the units.
- Inspections must include the examination of documented evidence that the supervisory controls in the monitoring plan have been performed and any indicated corrective action has been taken.
- Agreed upon procedures performed by internal auditing for the compliance officer are not audits; they are a consulting service.
- All compliance assurance work performed on the institution, regardless of external or internal source, should be coordinated by the compliance officer to avoid duplication of effort.

What about Noncompliance?

The primary purpose for implementing a compliance program in any institution is to minimize the instance of noncompliance with internal and external policies and procedures, laws, and rules and regulations (Chapter 10). There are two methods for minimizing noncompliance. One is the set of policies and procedures that governs the operation of each process in the organization. The other is a confidential reporting mechanism. Line management is responsible for the first method. The compliance program is responsible for the second method. Actions to achieve compliance, identification of noncompliance, and actions taken to prevent reoccurrence of noncompliance are all the responsibility of operating staff and management. If line management is to accept and carry out that responsibility, they must:

- Establish within each process's policies and procedures a "predefined set of consequences for noncompliance."
- Ensure that every employee in the process knows and understands the consequences of noncompliance.

- Ensure that any employee (administrator, faculty, or staff) suffers the prescribed consequences for instances of noncompliance.

Managing Those Risks not Currently Critical to the Institution

The compliance program, as described to this point, concentrates on managing those risks that can have a critical impact on the institution. The obvious question is, "What about all the other identified compliance risks?" (Chapter 11) Those risks also need to be managed using the same process that is used for institution critical risks. The difference with the other risks is in who provides the oversight control that the compliance function provides for the institutional risks. Table 13 presents a matrix that addresses this issue. The lesson learned is that compliance risks that are critical to any level of the organization should be managed at that level just as the institution critical risks are managed at the institution level. Among the many reasons for this is the simple one that any one of these other risks may become an institution critical risk at any moment. What comfort to know that it is already being managed.

How Did We Do? Where Do We Go from Here?

The final step in the implementation of a compliance program is a comparison of current status to the plan of action that established the program. This is usually accomplished through a self-assessment process. The results of that process dictate the next step. If the self-assessment is positive, then a validating external peer review would be performed. If the self-assessment is negative, the chief executive officer, the compliance officer, the compliance committee, and the other compliance program players need to revise the implementation plan. In either case, the final result is a new action plan. This is the end! This is the beginning!

Your Mission

An effective compliance program is a continuous process of plan, do, measure, learn, and plan. You are never done. However, the steps described in detail in the following pages will hopefully provide a useful guide for you while you are creating your own experience. Your contribution to this new body of knowledge will be to share your best practices, your pitfalls, and your program with others at future *Effective Compliance Systems* conferences.

INTRODUCTION

On March 20 and 21, 2001, a conference titled *Effective Compliance Systems* was held at the Joe C. Thompson Conference Center on the campus of The University of Texas at Austin in Austin, Texas. The conference was sponsored jointly by The Institute of Internal Auditors (IIA), the McCombs School of Business Center for Business Measurement and Assurance Services of The University of Texas at Austin, and The University of Texas System Audit Office. The *Effective Compliance Systems Conference* program is reproduced as Appendix A.

The catalyst for the conference was the external peer review of The University of Texas System Compliance Program and The University of Texas System Administration Compliance Program. As the peer review team was assembled, it became apparent that in all of higher education only The University of Texas System (U.T. System) had undertaken a comprehensive compliance program covering all aspects of both academic and health related operations. Shortly after the peer review report was issued, its findings were presented to the U.T. System-wide Compliance Committee and System-wide Compliance Officer. During the discussions of the report, it was suggested that the U.T. System might share what they had learned with other institutions of higher education in Texas and the nation. Urton Anderson, a member of the U.T. System-wide Compliance Committee and a professor of accounting and undergraduate dean in the McCombs School of Business, suggested that the McCombs School of Business might host such an event. Several months of discussion produced the joint venture that ultimately sponsored the conference.

The IIA provided the basic funding for the conference from an endowment established by Allen O. Hinkle. The McCombs School of Business, through its Center for Business Measurement and Assurance Services (BMAS), provided pre-conference registration, facilities coordination, funds management, and other essential support operations. The U.T. System Audit Office assembled the program and speakers and provided the support personnel on site at the conference.

The conference had 119 registrants and 30 presenters. The registrants and presenters came from all 16 U.T. component institutions, 11 institutions of higher education outside of Texas, three other Texas university systems, three independent institutions of higher education in Texas, four executive agencies in Texas, the Texas State Auditor's Office, two major consulting firms, and two small consulting firms.

As the idea of the conference matured, one of the main themes that received support was the development of a permanent body of knowledge from the conference. This theme will see fruition in this book, authored under the auspices of The IIA Research Foundation. The book contains the detailed elements of an effective compliance program as discussed by the various conference presenters and as implemented in The University of Texas Institutional Compliance Program. In addition to best practices and pitfalls, the book presents detailed examples of methodologies and forms used throughout the implementation of the U.T. System Institutional Compliance Program. There are also a number of appendices containing pertinent compliance information that was not presented at the conference.

You may read this book from cover to cover if you want a comprehensive picture of a compliance program. You may also read each chapter separately to gain information about a specific aspect of the compliance program, such as monitoring plans or confidential reporting mechanisms. It has been designed to be a reference for those whose fulltime effort is in the compliance program, and for those who only need information about a certain area of compliance that affects them.

The Institute of Internal Auditors Research Foundation

CHAPTER 1
LOSS OF FUNDING SOURCES!
LARGE FINES! IMAGE IMPAIRMENT!
WHY A COMPLIANCE PROGRAM

Nothing portrays more powerfully the need for an effective compliance system in an organization than a recital of instances of noncompliance that have been in the media and the negative impact they have had upon those institutions where they occurred. Table 1 is only a representative list of the most significant occurrences in the field of higher education during the past decade.

Table 1 Significant Instances of Noncompliance in Higher Education	
Noncompliance Issue	**Impact**
Allowable Costs on Federal Grants	$400,000+
Medicare Billing in Teaching Hospitals	$30,000,000
Cash Handling Procedures	$250,000
Employee/Contractor Classification – IRS	$1,000,000+
Account Reconciliation & Expenditure Control	$800,000
Player Eligibility – NCAA	Suspension of All Intercollegiate Athletics
Documentation of Billing for Medicare Charges	$20,000,000
Underage Student Alcohol Consumption	Student Death
Human Subjects in Research	Suspension of Research
Student Financial Aid Administration	Loss of All Federal Student Financial Aid Funds
Student Financial Aid Eligibility	$1,000,000+
Fire Hazards in Dormitories	$5,000,000+ Renovation Cost

Of course, it begins with Stanford University's alleged noncompliance with federal grant allowable cost regulations. It includes several other significant instances of alleged or actual noncompliance with regulations governing the use of federal funds, such as the University of Pennsylvania situation dealing with documentation when providing medical care at a teaching hospital. These cases usually result in a monetary loss, either through fines or reduced future funding to the organization, even when allegations are not proven. The list also contains several instances of noncompliance with laws and regulations, including those internal to the institution, which resulted in personal or financial harm to individuals and/or to the institutions where they occurred. In addition, all of these instances reflected negatively on the reputation of the institution involved. Regardless of the specific result of noncompliance, the institution in question spent precious management and staff time responding to allegations and doing damage control with their stakeholders.

The opening session of the *Effective Compliance Systems Conference* was a panel presentation by representatives of the three institutions who are pioneers in the field of compliance systems in higher education. The objective of their presentations was to make the audience aware of the fact that compliance issues can touch anyone and they can have a significant negative impact upon an institution. The panelists, Steve Jung, Internal Audit Director and newly appointed Compliance Officer of Stanford University, Odell Guyton, Corporate Compliance Officer of the University of Pennsylvania, and Charles G. Chaffin, Director of Audits and System-wide Compliance Officer of The University of Texas System, talked about their specific instances of noncompliance and the impact upon their institutions and upon higher education in general.

The Stanford University Compliance Experience: It's Bad

The theme of Jung's presentation was that compliance is necessary because we cannot stand the consequences of noncompliance. (See Table 2 for his summary of those consequences.)

Table 2 Consequences of Noncompliance
• Fines, penalties, and legal fees
• Media coverage and blemished reputation
• Imposed compliance "settlements"
• More regulatory and audit agency scrutiny
• Management time and effort required to perform damage control
• Management turnover
• Lower faculty and staff morale
• Increased bureaucracy and lower efficiency
• Lingering effects.......
• Guilt by association: when one of us is tarred, we all wear the features

As an example of consequences, he discussed the impact upon Stanford of the federal government allegation that unallowable costs were being charged to federal grants. The "Stanford Yacht" case, so called because some of the alleged unallowable expenses were for operation of a yacht owned by the university, cost Stanford University several hundred thousand dollars, even though they never admitted guilt. This was the first highly publicized instance in higher education where an institution had to reimburse a funds provider because of failure to comply with conditions attached to the receipt of funds. In addition, there was a consequence for all of higher education when the federal government, as a result of the Stanford case, placed a cap on the percent of indirect cost that could be charged to a grant.

It is interesting to note that Stanford University did not establish a compliance program as a result of this case. Instead, they choose to strengthen the controls surrounding the operation and financial accounting for grants and contracts, and to strengthen the internal auditing function.   Only in late 2000 and early 2001, in response to new instances of noncompliance, did Stanford University begin the implementation of a comprehensive institutional compliance program.   Stanford's institutional compliance plan is shown as Appendix D.

The University of Pennsylvania Compliance Experience: It Gets Worse

Odell Guyton followed with a very appropriate discussion of the next major compliance case in higher education; the University of Pennsylvania PATH (Physicians at Teaching Hospitals) audit in 1994. He discussed the federal government's allegation that the university was inappropriately billing Medicare for services of interns and teaching physicians. In other words, they were failing to comply with Medicare regulations in billing for services. The original recovery amount sought by the government was approximately $100 million and the university settled with the federal government for $30 million.

The University of Pennsylvania moved a step farther down the path to a comprehensive compliance program than Stanford had done. They immediately sought to mitigate their future risk by implementing a corporate compliance program concentrating on their hospital related activities. A corporate compliance function was established and Lisa Murtha was employed as the first corporate compliance officer in an institution of higher education. The essential ingredients of a compliance program were established and applied to those issues where federal funding and hospital operations intersected. In 2000, the University of Pennsylvania was hit with new allegations of noncompliance with federal regulations in an area unrelated to hospital operations, namely, human subjects in research. He presented a review of the results of those allegations. The most serious alleged result of noncompliance was the loss of a patient's life. In addition, the specific research in question was halted and other research projects were suspended until the university could show evidence of a framework for compliance. Once again, the impact upon higher education was dramatic as other research universities were subjected to increased oversight of human subject projects. In fact, this incident has resulted in selected human subject research being suspended for various lengths of time in several major universities around the country.

The University of Texas System Compliance Experience: It's Everywhere

Charles G. Chaffin was the final presenter in this opening session. His litany of compliance failures dates from the early 1990s. Included was noncompliance with university policies and procedures as well as external laws and regulations. Loss of revenues, damaged reputation, major lifetime exposure to lawsuits and damages, and increased scrutiny by federal funding agencies were all described in his presentation. The earliest of these instances involved noncompliance with internal U.T. System policies and procedures. Responses to these instances of compliance failure resulted in corrective actions only in the affected processes.

This targeted response did little to affect compliance in other areas of activity. Noncompliance with Internal Revenue Service rules governing the classification of a worker as employee or contractor and with local and state fire safety codes in laboratory buildings resulted in fines and negative media exposure. The Board of Regents of the U.T. System responded to these new instances of noncompliance with a demand for a more comprehensive solution. In 1994, U.T. System reacted to its latest compliance problems with the inauguration of an initiative aimed at a systemic correction: the training of all managers, academic and administrative, on the full range of their financial, operational, and compliance responsibilities. This effort was spearheaded by the U.T. System Internal Audit Office under Chaffin and reached all 4,000 managers within the U.T. System. The program was perceived as being highly successful.

However, in December 1997, one of the health-related U.T. System components was charged with improperly billing Medicare and was presented with a multi-million dollar assessment. Obviously, three years of effort had not produced the desired results of controlling surprises in the compliance arena. Charles Chaffin described very clearly the reaction of the U.T. System Board of Regents. The chairman asked for assurance that systems were in place to prevent future situations at all of the components. Of course, no such assurance could be given. As Chaffin relates it, that answer caused the chairman, with support of the entire board, to order the immediate implementation of a comprehensive institutional compliance program grounded in management providing proactive, ongoing assurance regarding compliance with all laws, rules, regulations, policies, and procedures applicable to the U.T. System.

Can You Afford to Have a Compliance Experience?

Loss of Funding Sources! Large Fines! Image Impairment! These are the fruits of noncompliance. The possibility of any one of these outcomes should cause every board member and every executive in an institution of higher education to seriously consider the implementation of an effective compliance system for their institution. In fact, more and more institutions are seriously exploring the implementation of such systems as a hedge against maximum monetary damages and unretractable media exposure. The problem that these institutions are discovering, though, is that there are few models of operating compliance systems in higher education.

The University of Texas System, which has examples of both external noncompliance and institutional noncompliance in its history, looked for higher education compliance system models to follow when it began its implementation three years ago. The only one available then was the University of Pennsylvania model that dealt almost exclusively with hospital issues involving federal funds. However, The University of Texas System Board of Regents was not interested in just hospital issues; they wanted a comprehensive compliance system that covered all significant compliance risks. As a consequence, The University of Texas System had to develop its own model for a comprehensive compliance system. In the succeeding sessions of the conference the highlights of that model were presented. In the following chapters, the information provided by the conference presenters will be expanded with detailed explanations of the design and implementation process, including forms and reports, best practices, and pitfalls.

Welcome to The University of Texas System Institutional Compliance Program!

CHAPTER 2
THE ESSENTIAL ELEMENTS OF AN EFFECTIVE COMPLIANCE SYSTEM

Being aware of the consequences of noncompliance is not enough. The higher education executive must become familiar with the essential elements of a compliance system designed to mitigate negative exposures for the institution. This chapter will acquaint you with the essential elements of any compliance system, and it will compare those elements to the elements of COSO, the most widely used internal control model in the United States.

U.S. Sentencing Guidelines

The elements of a successful compliance program were outlined by Odell Guyton of the University of Pennsylvania in the opening session of the second day of the *Effective Compliance Systems Conference*. The information he presented was based upon the compliance program model in the *U.S. Sentencing Guidelines for Organizations* (United States Sentencing Commission, Guidelines Manual, &8A1.2 (November 1991)). That model lists seven requirements. The fifth requirement of that model contains two very distinct and significant requirements, so we present them here separately, resulting in eight essential requirements for a successful compliance program:

1. Establish compliance standards and procedures to be followed by employees and other agents.
2. Assign high-level personnel to have overall responsibility for overseeing compliance with such standards and procedures.
3. Use care to avoid delegating substantial discretionary authority to individuals whom the organization knows, or should have reason to know, have a propensity to engage in illegal activities.
4. Effectively communicate the standards and procedures to all employees by requiring participation in training and by disseminating publications that explain in understandable language what is required.
5. A. Take reasonable steps to achieve compliance with standards by utilizing monitoring and auditing systems that have been designed to reasonably detect noncompliance.
5. B. Provide and publicize a system for employees and other agents to report suspected noncompliance without fear of retaliation (confidential reporting system).
6. Consistently enforce the standards through appropriate disciplinary mechanisms.
7. Take all reasonable steps to respond appropriately to detected offenses and to prevent future similar offenses.

The Institute of Internal Auditors Research Foundation

A little history about the *U.S. Sentencing Guidelines* and companion federal laws will certainly help put these requirements in perspective.

The U. S. Sentencing Commission was created in 1984 and the Guidelines were promulgated in November 1991. The primary purpose of the sentencing guidelines, one for organizations and one for individuals, was to provide uniformity of sentencing for those found guilty of violation of federal laws. Recognizing that rewards can be better motivators than punishments, the U.S. Sentencing Commission outlined a punishment structure based upon both the seriousness of the offense and the actions taken by the organization to help prevent the offense. The vehicle to be utilized by an organization to demonstrate a proactive approach to minimizing criminal activity (noncompliance) was a corporate compliance program that included, as a minimum, the eight elements listed above. While the Commission did not require organizations to design and implement a compliance program that includes these eight elements, it did provide a very practical incentive for doing that. The incentive was that an organization found guilty of violating federal criminal laws (usually the result of noncompliance with a federal statute) could reduce its assessed penalties by up to 70 percent of the fines required by law if the organization could demonstrate it had an acceptable compliance program. What higher education executive would not want the ability to reduce a $100 million fine to under $30 million?

These Guidelines were issued after the "Stanford yacht" incident and some of the early U.T. System noncompliance issues. Higher education generally viewed the Guidelines as affecting only commercial corporations, but this changed with the University of Pennsylvania PATH audit settlement in December 1995. It became very clear at that time that higher education could be subjected to the same rules as corporations, especially in the area of violating federal statutes, basically the False Claims Act. Applicability became even clearer with the passage of the Health Insurance and Accountability Act of 1996, which provided significant funding and authority to both the Justice Department and the Department of Health and Human Services Office of Inspector General to find and punish health-care fraud. Because of the level of federal funding in higher education, colleges and universities, especially those with medical related activities, became a fertile field for federal agency enforcement and recovery initiatives. The transfer of emphasis from medical related federal funding to all federal funding was just a matter of time, and has, in fact, already occurred.

The Relationship Between the Guidelines and the
COSO Control Model

Now that we are aware of what must be included in a compliance program, let's examine how that program relates to what we should already be doing in our organizations in the way of control systems. Those institutions of higher education that have already adopted the COSO Internal Control Model will find that their compliance program can build upon and greatly enhance that control model. In fact, the approach that the U.T. System has taken with their compliance program is to integrate it into the COSO model and to redefine that model. This process will be explained in the appropriate chapters that follow.

For the moment, we will demonstrate the relationship between the compliance program expressed in the Guidelines and the COSO control system that should already be in place through use of the comparisons used by Odell Guyton during his presentation. The COSO model has five areas of activity: Control Environment, Risk Assessment, Control Activities, Information and Communication, and Monitoring.

- The Control Environment is defined as "The Tone at the Top," or the ethical values and operating philosophy of the organization as defined and practiced by management. In the Guidelines' requirements this concept is expressed in these elements:
  - ➢ Establish standards and procedures.
  - ➢ Assign high-level personnel to oversee the program.
  - ➢ Avoid delegation of discretionary authority to personnel with propensity for criminal activity.
  - ➢ Consistently enforce sanctions.
- Risk assessment is defined in COSO as the identification and analysis of relevant risks to achievement of the goals and objectives of the institution. The essential elements of a successful compliance program that address this area of activity are:
  - ➢ Take reasonable steps to achieve compliance (identify compliance risks.
  - ➢ Take all reasonable steps to prevent future noncompliance events (analyze noncompliance events to determine validity of risk assessment).
- Control activities are the policies and procedures that help ensure management directives are carried out. The Guidelines elements that reflect this COSO activity are:
  - ➢ Establish standards and procedures to be followed by employees and other agents.
  - ➢ Take reasonable steps to achieve compliance with the standards and procedures through use of monitoring and auditing systems.
- The information and communication activity area in COSO deals with (1) providing each employee all of the information needed to carry out assigned duties and (2) providing avenues for employees to both receive and provide information necessary to the effective operation of the organization. The requirements of the Guidelines that support this activity area are:
  - ➢ Effectively communicate the standards and procedures to all employees through training and understandable publications that explain what is required.
  - ➢ Provide and publicize a system for employees and other agents to report suspected noncompliance without fear of retaliation (confidential reporting system).

The Institute of Internal Auditors Research Foundation

- Monitoring is a process that assesses the quality of a system's performance over time. The monitoring may be ongoing, that is activities performed by management as a part of operations, or periodic, that is activities performed outside of operations by internal or external auditors or other external evaluators. The Guidelines address this activity area in the following essential element:
  - ➢ Take reasonable steps to achieve compliance with standards by utilizing monitoring and auditing systems that have been designed to reasonably detect noncompliance.

This brief comparison of the activity areas of COSO and the essential elements of a successful compliance system clearly demonstrates that an effective compliance program is really not a new initiative. It is simply a strengthening of the risk mitigation and control structures that should already be in place in your institution.

Consequently, a successful compliance system is not a new administrative requirement for your institution. It is an emphasis on what should already be in place. In fact, if the COSO control model had been implemented by all members of the higher education community when it was adopted in the early 1990s, we, as an industry, would not be facing the prospect now of implementing compliance programs. The theme that "a successful compliance program is nothing new, it is just the way business should have always been done in higher education," will appear over and over in the succeeding chapters. A successful compliance system is simply GOOD BUSINESS, nothing more.

We know why we need a compliance program. We know what that program must include and how it fits into our overall operations as an organization. So, how do we actually go about designing and implementing the program that is right for our unique institution? Keep reading!

CHAPTER 3
HOW TO START:
AN ACTION PLAN TO
ENHANCE COMPLIANCE

The immediate question that usually comes to mind, once you are convinced of the necessity of a compliance program and understand what it should include, is "How do we get started"? Scott Scarborough, the Chief Business Officer and Compliance Officer at The University of Texas at Tyler, discussed the U.T. System approach to answering that question in his presentation closing the first day of the conference. He emphasized the key ingredients for such an effort; namely, inclusion of representatives from all constituencies on the ad hoc committee to design the program, acquisition of all relevant information for making decisions, and adoption of an operating philosophy (mission statement), goals, and objectives. The output from this activity will be the road map for implementation of your compliance program. This chapter outlines how the U.T. System developed their road map, *An Action Plan to Ensure Institutional Compliance*, and what they would have done differently after attempting to follow that road map for three years. The discussion is divided into the development of the action plan and the action plan.

Development of the Action Plan

The Ad Hoc Committee to Design the Compliance Program

The first order of business, once the decision is made to have a compliance program, is to establish a committee to develop the program. Generally, this will be an ad hoc committee that functions only until a plan is developed and accepted. The most important feature of this committee is that it must include appropriate representation from all facets of the institutional community. To accomplish this goal of inclusiveness, the executive management of the institution must ensure that the committee includes an appropriate number of appointees representing faculty, medical staff (if there are medical operations), professionals, administrative areas, students, and, perhaps, even contractors who provide services in the institutional environment (outsourced operations).

In the U.T. System experience the chief executive officer asked his executive management team to submit names of persons in their areas of authority who would be appropriate to serve on the committee. Since the culture of the U.T. System saw compliance as a business issue, most of the members of the ad hoc committee were business officers or officials from the administrative activities of the system. Even in the medical areas of activity, the representatives on the committee tended to be from the business side of those operations. This does not mean that the action plan produced was basically flawed. It would probably have been the same regardless of the composition of the ad hoc committee that produced it. However, because of the makeup of that committee, most members of the institutional community initially viewed the compliance program as a business area program with medical activity implications.

As we look at the U.T. System experience, we must remember that there was no model in higher education to follow. The only compliance program in existence in 1998 in higher education involved hospital and medical school activity. With no pattern to follow and no previous experiences to learn from, the U.T. System compliance program had to carve out a new process — the comprehensive institutional compliance process. At times the road has been straight and first decisions have proved to be the optimal decisions. At other times, like the composition of the ad hoc committee that began it all, the initial track has proved less than optimal and, consequently, has been revised to eliminate obstacles.

Lesson Learned:

Faculty and other groups that may have resistance to the program must be included on the committee designing the compliance program. This accomplishes two main objectives. First, it ensures that all groups of the covered community have ownership in the compliance program through a group member who can be the champion for compliance within that group. Second, it provides every group with a vehicle for expressing their concerns, frustrations, and objections to the program early in its development so that appropriate attention can be given to overcoming those negative reactions before the program implementation begins. In the U.T. System, broad inclusive membership was not one of the criteria in appointing the ad hoc committee. As a result, considerable resistance from faculty, doctors, and others outside of the business affairs arena created a diversion from the main thrust of the program for its first three years of existence.

Acquisition of All Pertinent Information to Make Decisions About a Compliance Program

The ad hoc committee began meeting immediately after its appointment in late January 1998. The committee was chaired by a member of the executive management team and was provided with operational support from the U.T. System Audit Office. The first task was to gather all the information available about an effective compliance program. The *U.S. Sentencing Guidelines,* the *False Claims Act,* and the *Health Insurance and Accountability Act of 1996* and guidelines of the Office of Inspector General of the Department of Health and Human Services were all assembled and reviewed. (Appendix C provides a comparison of the 16 steps in the U.T. System action plan to the requirements of both the *U.S. Sentencing Guidelines* and the Office of Inspector General, Department of Health and Human Services, Guidelines for Hospitals.) However, the committee found that there was also an increasingly large body of regulatory and legal actions relating to compliance that needed to be considered in developing a successful compliance program. As the volume of information to be digested became clear, the committee and its support staff made the decision to seek outside help from someone who might be knowledgeable in the compliance area.

At the time of these activities — January and February 1998 — it was fairly easy to identify the primary source of information in the compliance area. That source was the former corporate compliance officer for the University of Pennsylvania, Lisa Murtha. Lisa had taken her compliance expertise gained at Penn and joined the consulting services function in an international auditing and consulting firm. Beginning in early March 1998, she and her colleagues provided the external help that the U.T. System needed to sift through all of the information available and produce an effective action plan. Lisa served as educator, resource person, and facilitator during the development process.

The information-gathering phase can be intimidating as the volume of information available on compliance systems expands. A bibliography of pertinent printed material available at the time of this writing is included. However, you must keep two things in mind when you use that bibliography; first, by the time you read it, it is no longer current, and, second, only parts of the information available at any time may be pertinent to your institution.

Lesson Learned:

You need help to begin an effective compliance program. That help can come from outside consultants, whether from large auditing/consulting firms or from smaller firms dealing specifically with the college and university market. However, it can also come from other colleges and universities who are willing to share their experiences in the compliance arena. The University of Texas System offers its expertise and services in implementing compliance programs to any institution of higher education requesting them. As time passes, there will certainly be others who will offer such services to their peers. The purpose of this book is to provide a documented approach to implementing an effective compliance system that would be available to and affordable for every organization in higher education.

Table 3 is a summary of the steps in the development of an action plan.

The Institute of Internal Auditors Research Foundation

Table 3
Action Plan Development Steps

1. Appoint an ad hoc committee to design the action plan and compliance program.

2. Educate the ad hoc committee concerning what is an acceptable compliance program

3. Adopt an operating philosophy and goals and objectives for the compliance program

4. Draft the action plan for the compliance program

5. Obtain approval of the action plan

Adoption of an Operating Philosophy, Goals, and Objectives for the Compliance Program

With the information gathered by the support team and interpreted by the outside consultants, the committee produced a draft action plan during March 1998. The first sentence of the Introduction expressed the operating philosophy of the compliance program, namely, to ensure U.T. System compliance with applicable laws, regulations, policies, and procedures. There are no limiting descriptors, no exclusions concerning applicable laws, regulations, policies, and procedures. Everything is covered. It is universal, comprehensive. It includes not only specified laws and the interpretations of those laws (regulations), but also internal rules (policies and procedures). It is also significant with regard to policies and procedures that no distinction is made between those that carry Regent authority and those that carry operating management authority. The key concept is inclusiveness. This program applies to everyone in every aspect of the institution's life.

While the specific goals and objectives of the compliance program are detailed in the action plan, the general goal or objective is clearly stated in the Introduction's first sentence in the phrase "ensure U.T. System compliance." During all of the activity in this development period, from the chairman's call to action to the presentation of the plan to the Board of Regents, the emphasis was on ensuring compliance. The consultants and the data available in the literature reinforced this. Consequently, the goal included the word "ensure." However, in reviewing the activities that occurred in developing the action plan, it is clear that the intent of the ad hoc committee was to provide a proactive program that minimized noncompliance. It is simply unfortunate that the concept was labeled as "ensure" compliance.

Lesson Learned:

Choose the words you use in describing your compliance program with great care. Be sure they reflect exactly what you intend to convey. Ambiguity can detract from the achievement of program goals and objectives. Unrealistic expectations can also impact the achievable results of the program. Individuals may look at the word "ensure" and conclude that it can never be attained; therefore, why try. In other words, don't create unnecessary obstacles to the compliance program through poor choice of words. There are enough real obstacles.

The Action Plan

The Approval Process

Once agreement on these issues was achieved the actual writing of the action plan was delegated to one member of the committee, Scott Scarborough. The draft plan that he produced was then discussed, revised, and approved by the full committee. The committee submitted it to the chief executive officer of the U.T. System who presented it to all of the executive management team (including presidents of the 16 component institutions) of the U.T. System during the first few weeks of April. The draft was also presented to the chairman of the Business Affairs and Audit Committee of the Board of Regents. Finally, the *Action Plan to Ensure Institutional Compliance* was presented to the Business Affairs and Audit Committee of the Board on April 24, 1998, and, at that time, became the road map for the U.T. System Institutional Compliance Program.

Lesson Learned:

Hindsight indicates that a formal resolution creating the U.T. System Institutional Compliance Program would have provided additional authority and emphasis to the program. A formal Board of Regents resolution adopting the *Action Plan to Ensure Institutional Compliance* did not accompany the plan when it was presented to the Business Affairs and Audit Committee of the Board of Regents. Consequently, the Board of Regents acted upon no formal document adopting the plan until almost three years into the program.

Action Plan Objectives

The *Action Plan to Ensure Institutional Compliance* in The University of Texas System is reproduced in its entirety as Appendix B. The Introduction to that document is a concise summary of the plan's key objectives with associated key responsibilities and accountabilities. When you review Appendix B to find the detail for each of the 16 objectives in the action plan, you will notice that the plan states each objective, who is responsible for each objective, and completion dates for each objective. When the action plan was developed, the committee believed that the program could be implemented within one year and the due dates for completion of each objective reflected that philosophy.

Lesson Learned:

The implementation of an effective compliance system at any institution or system of institutions can take up to five years, perhaps longer. The actual length of the implementation period depends upon the culture of the institution. A comprehensive, effective compliance program requires a culture change at any institution, some a major change, and others a minor one. At any rate, because of the culture change factor, implementation can cover a long time period. As you develop your compliance action plan, assess the culture of your institution and estimate how much it has to change for the compliance program to become a part of the daily fabric of the institution. Then, and only then, set your target completion dates for each objective.

Action Plan Responsibility and Accountability

The responsibility and accountability structure of the action plan is represented by the organization chart in Figure 1.

Every employee in the U.T. System has a responsibility in the compliance program. Accountability begins with the lowest level supervisor and extends through all levels of management to the Board of Regents.

- The chief administrative officer is responsible and accountable to the chancellor for:
  - ➢ Providing adequate resources for the compliance program.
  - ➢ Taking appropriate action on noncompliance.
- The compliance officer is responsible and accountable to the chief administrative officer for:
  - ➢ Establishing and maintaining a risk process that builds compliance consciousness into daily activities, monitors the effectiveness of those processes, and communicates noncompliance to appropriate administrators for corrective action.
  - ➢ Filing a risk-based plan and quarterly activity reports with the system-wide compliance officer.
- The compliance committee is responsible and accountable to the compliance officer for:
  - ➢ Providing guidance and direction to the program.
  - ➢ Providing follow-up on actions taken on noncompliance.

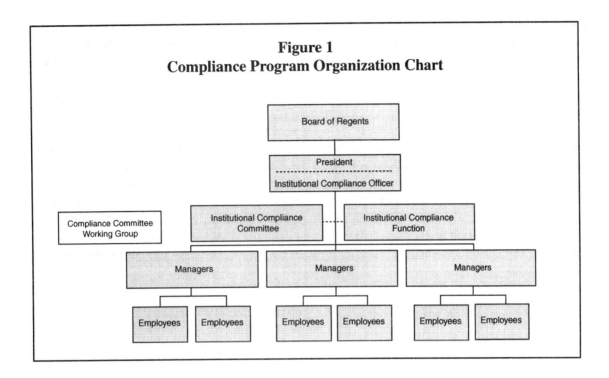

Figure 1
Compliance Program Organization Chart

- The compliance office/function is responsible and accountable to the compliance officer for:
  - ➢ Providing training.
  - ➢ Determining effectiveness of monitoring.
  - ➢ Preparing reports.
- Internal audit is responsible and accountable to the chief administrative officer and the Board of Regents for:
  - ➢ Auditing the risk-based plan for design and effectiveness.
- Every manager at all levels is accountable for compliance in their operational unit, whether it is a work group, a department, a college or school, or the institution.
- Every employee is responsible for the actual compliance with laws, regulations, policies, and procedures applicable to the performance of their job.

The Institute of Internal Auditors Research Foundation

Lesson Learned:

Compliance has to be made relevant to each employee. Each employee must be able to see why the minimization of instances of noncompliance is important to them on a personal level. You may get their attention by appealing to their sense of duty and loyalty to the institution or its students; but if you want each employee to proactively think about and do something to control compliance risk, it is necessary to demonstrate to each the individual implications of noncompliance. Most resistance to a compliance program comes from employees who believe that they will not be affected by the negative consequences of noncompliance. Once they see that their lives can be negatively affected, even when they are innocent, resistance fades.

You are now ready to enter into the implementation stage of a compliance program. The remainder of this book is divided into chapters dealing with the implementation of the essential elements of a compliance program. Some of those elements will require multiple chapters and you will be so advised when that happens. For some elements, there will also be additional chapters which explain enhancements to the basic compliance process which were developed within the U.T. System to handle issues not previously addressed in compliance programs or issues unique to systems of higher education with multiple, semi-autonomous components. Once again, these chapters will be appropriately identified so that you can determine whether or not they apply to your situation.

CHAPTER 4
THE CHIEF EXECUTIVE OFFICER: KEYSTONE OF AN EFFECTIVE COMPLIANCE PROGRAM

Chief executives from three of the 16 institutions within the U.T. System and R.D. Burck, the Chancellor of The University of Texas System, provided insight into the role of the chief executive officer in an effective compliance program. Their universal theme was that active participation of the chief executive officer is a prerequisite to the success of a compliance program. A condensation of their presentations provides a very complete outline of the activities required of the chief executive officer whose institution is embarking on the implementation of a compliance program. The five activities are presented in Table 4.

Table 4
Chief Executive Officer Activities

- **Assimilate** the compliance processes into the institution's daily life.

- **Participate** in the compliance program through example and visibility.

- **Communicate** with the institutional community, individual employees, and the board.

- **Allocate** time, skills, and dollars to the compliance program.

- **Validate** the process by ensuring appropriate consequences for noncompliance.

Lesson Learned

The chief executive officer of the institution must become the compliance program champion at the institution.

The Institute of Internal Auditors Research Foundation

Assimilate

The institution's CEO must assimilate compliance into the daily fabric of institutional life for it to become effective in mitigating noncompliance and eliminating surprises. The key to this assimilation is a realization on the part of the CEO that a compliance program can enhance the management process of the institution. As the CEO realizes that the tools used to manage compliance risk are the same tools that are needed to manage all risks of the institution, it becomes very clear that an effective compliance process can significantly impact the entire management process.

Lesson Learned

An effective compliance program has a positive impact on the overall management process of an institution. In his dinner remarks on the first day of the conference, Robert Witt, President of The University of Texas at Arlington, made this point very clear. He indicated it was not until he realized the full impact an effective compliance program could have upon all the other risk areas of his university, operating and financial and reporting, that he really embraced the program. It was then that he seriously began the process of participation, communication, allocation, and validation so that every employee of his university would know how important the compliance program was. His charge to other CEOs was to recognize the power that an effective compliance program brought to their management process and to harness that power for success — not just in compliance, but in the achievement of all the institution's goals and objectives. The charge was to assimilate compliance (that is risk management) into the day-to-day life of the institution.

Participate

Chief executive officers actively participate in the compliance process in three ways. They (1) lead by example, (2) emphasize "doing the right thing," and (3) are visible.

Lead by Example

"If the boss can do it, so can I." Employees watch the chief executive officer to determine what is and is not allowed in the operations of the institution. A chief executive officer who personally complies with all the laws, regulations, policies, and procedures that affect the institution can reasonably expect everyone else connected with the institution to do the same. However, if the chief executive bends the rules for himself or herself or for friends, then everyone else will believe they are entitled to do the same. In the COSO control model used by organizations, commercial and not-for-profit, in the United States this is called the control environment of the organization. In order for any compliance program to be effective, the control environment set by the chief executive officer must be one of adherence to all appropriate laws, regulations, policies, and procedures. The chief executive officer sets the standard of performance in the compliance arena.

Emphasize "Doing the Right Thing"

The chief executive must make a "big deal" out of the concept of "doing the right thing." Discussion of this concept should be in every document the chief executive issues regarding the operating philosophy of the institution. There should also be prescribed and visible consequences when an employee violates this concept of operations. "Doing the right thing" has been defined as (1) complying with all applicable laws, regulations, policies, and procedures, and (2) acting with equity toward all parties in a transaction. The institution's chief executive must continuously emphasize to employees that "doing the right thing" is an integral part of the institution's operating philosophy. Knowing what constitutes "doing the right thing" is a function of the general and specialized training components of an effective compliance program. However, Burck suggests in his written remarks that there is a universal approach to being sure you are doing the right thing. That approach is to simply ask yourself if your institution would be ashamed or embarrassed by your actions were they to appear as headlines on tomorrow's news. It is the chief executive officer's responsibility to keep this concept constantly on the minds of all employees.

Be Visible

The chief executive officer must personally participate in significant compliance events such as compliance committee meetings, general training events, peer reviews, and awareness campaigns. The staff of any institution, from senior management to custodians, recognizes that there are many issues that demand the time of the chief executive officer. They also recognize that the chief executive only devotes time to those issues that he or she believes are important to the successful management of the institution. Consequently, when fellow employees see the chief executive attending the various compliance events, they know that compliance is important. This influences everyone to make managing compliance risk an important part of regular job duties.

Communicate

An inseparable partner of participation is communication, the selling of the compliance program to the institutional community. The chief executive officer who is effective in this area uses three approaches: (1) general messages to all employees, (2) specific messages of praise or chastisement for individuals or groups of employees, and (3) reports to the governing board.

General Messages to Employees

An example of general messages to employees is the yearly statement of operating philosophy, which is sent to each U.T. System employee by their chief executive officer. This is a positive statement of the operating philosophy of the institution and includes heavy emphasis on "doing the right thing." Besides this annual reminder to all employees, the chief executive officer delivers a videotaped message to all new employees about the operating philosophy and compliance as a part of New Employee Orientation. Finally, the chief executive ensures the importance of the compliance program by communicating to all employees the requirement for annual general compliance training.

Specific Messages of Praise and Chastisement

As appropriate, the chief executive officer should recognize those employees who have prevented, through the exercise of their assigned responsibilities, instances of noncompliance that would have been detrimental to the institution. These accolades communicate appreciation for work well done and become a very effective motivator for future successes. They also give the chief executive officer an opportunity to demonstrate concrete benefits from the considerable effort required for an effective compliance program. However, one-dimensional communication can produce cynicism. So, the chief executive officer must, when appropriate, call attention to the compliance failures of staff, both senior and otherwise, which have put the institution at risk. One purpose of this type of message is to let everyone know that noncompliance is not acceptable and can result in personal embarrassment or worse. More important, though, it can serve as a vehicle for the chief executive to reinforce the importance of compliance and its affect upon the entire institution. In either case, praise or chastisement, whether it is done in public or private, word usually filters throughout the organization and reinforces the importance of "doing the right thing."

Report to the Board

The compliance program should always be on the chief executive officer's agenda for discussion with the governing board of the institution. The governing board is ultimately responsible for the success or failure of the organization and has an inherent interest in the effective management of risk. Their personal interest in how compliance risk is managed can contribute greatly to the success of the program. That interest is expressed through receiving reports of program status from the chief executive officer and providing direction and encouragement to the chief executive officer. It is primarily evidenced by inclusion of compliance as a regular item for board action. Support of the governance function is a necessary corollary to proactive chief executive officer involvement in the compliance program.

Communication, then, includes telling everyone what is expected of them concerning compliance, personally addressing the extremes of compliance behavior, and keeping the governing board informed of all that is happening in the compliance area.

Lesson Learned

The message must be delivered over and over. Once is not enough, with employees or with the governing board. An effective compliance program involves a culture change for the majority of institutions in higher education. Constant communication in varied forms and media is a precursor of success.

Allocate

Through participation and communication, the chief executive officer demonstrates commitment to the compliance program. That commitment will not be fruitful unless it is support by an allocation of resources for the program. The chief executive officer must provide the appropriate amount of three types of resources to the compliance program if it is to be effective. Those three types of resources are employee time, current staff with special skills, and dollars.

Employee Time

The chief executive officer must make compliance activities a task in every employee's job description. Accomplishment of compliance responsibilities must become a component of the evaluation process for every employee, including senior management, middle and first-line managers, and all staff. In this way, the chief executive makes compliance a normal part of each job rather than a special, additional responsibility. This is the only way to ensure that managers and employees are provided appropriate time to attend both general and specialized training, to participate in risk assessment and mitigation activities, and to serve on committees and assurance teams. If this allocation of time is not made, everyone in the institutional community will view compliance activities as something that takes time away from their normal duties, so either normal duties or compliance will suffer.

Lesson Learned

The allocation of employee time to the compliance program is significant. Witt, President of The University of Texas at Arlington, estimates that employees at his institution spent over 10,000 man-hours in compliance activities during the first two years of implementation and operation.

Current Staff with Special Skills

The allocation of resources that the chief executive officer must make involves current staff with special skills. During the implementation phase of a compliance program, the most practical and efficient way to implement the program may be through the efforts of staff who currently work in areas other than compliance. There are many functions within an institution of higher education that deal with compliance risk management, such as internal auditing, environmental health and safety, intercollegiate athletics, hospital operations, and others. The chief executive officer must be willing to draw upon the skills and resources of these operations to staff the fledgling compliance function until it takes root and the extent of its operation is determined. Recognition of the transferability of skills from specific compliance to universal compliance is essential in making this allocation. Individual department considerations must be subordinated to the overall health and success of the institution.

Lesson Learned

Use of current staff to populate the startup compliance function should be a temporary solution. Once the compliance program is established and an informed decision is made by the chief executive officer on the appropriate organization of the compliance function, permanent staff should be assigned, if appropriate. This does not preclude employees of other departments who are assigned temporarily to the compliance function from becoming permanent compliance function employees. It simply means they must severe their association with their home department to avoid conflict of interest issues. The most prominent area of concern is the use of internal auditing staff or department as the temporary compliance function during implementation.

Dollars

The final allocation of resources available to the chief executive is the allocation of dollars or budget authority. The appropriate budget for the compliance function depends upon the compliance environment of the institution. A chief executive officer whose institution includes medical teaching or treatment facilities and significant research activities would probably have a larger compliance function budget than an institution that engages mainly in undergraduate instruction. There is no one answer. The chief executive officer with the governing board should determine the appropriate budget.

Lesson Learned

The budget for compliance may include both funds that were previously budgeted elsewhere to perform specific compliance functions and new funds for the compliance function. New funds would be resources that had previously been devoted to some other aspect of the organization. This allocation of new funds can cause considerable resentment within the institutional community unless the chief executive officer has carefully laid the foundation for a compliance function through assimilation, participation, communication, allocation, and, the final action, validation.

Validate

Validation is the act of closing the loop in the compliance program. The chief executive officer who is involved intimately in the program, who communicates to all their responsibilities in the program, who allocates appropriate resources to carry out the program, must finally ensure that something positive is the result of all this activity. This validation involves (1) keeping informed about instances of significant potential or actual noncompliance, (2) ensuring that like instances of noncompliance receive like consequences, (3) ensuring consequences of instances of noncompliance are appropriate to the situation, and (4) sharing what is learned from each instance of noncompliance.

Keeping Informed

Probably the easiest of the four activities in validation is keeping informed about instances of significant potential or actual noncompliance. The chief executive officer has two avenues to accomplish this objective: (1) written periodic reports, and (2) oral, as-needed reports. The written, periodic report is an efficient way to review status of activities and the results of actions taken on noncompliance. The oral, as-needed report is the most effective way to avoid noncompliance surprises.

Lesson Learned

The chief executive officer must create an atmosphere of openness and trust within the institution if oral, as-needed reporting is to be effective. Senior managers, line managers, and employees will not come forward with potential problem areas unless they are confident their concerns will be addressed objectively. A successful compliance program requires trust, empowerment, and respect for all employees. It requires an open line of communication both up and down the institutional organization.

Ensure that Like Instances of Noncompliance Receive Like Consequences

For all of the employees of an institution to become willing and active participants in minimizing noncompliance instances, they must know that the senior manager who does not comply will receive the same consequences as the custodian who does not comply. They must know that the faculty member who does not comply receives the same consequences as the administrator who does not comply. It is the chief executive officer's responsibility to see that this equity of consequence exists in the program and is demonstrated in the actions taken on noncompliance. This is a difficult task for the chief executive since vary few situations are exactly alike, even though they appear to be alike.

Lesson Learned

The chief executive officer must very early in the program establish a mechanism for evaluating the equity of consequences of noncompliance. The mechanism must include a review process for evaluating the facts of each situation and the potential or realized risk to the institution from each situation, and the relationship of the consequences to both of these factors. It must also include a methodology for disseminating information to the institutional community on the results of the review process.

Ensuring Consequences are Appropriate to the Situation

In addition to treating all levels of the organization the same, the CEO needs to also ensure that the consequence for a particular instance of noncompliance fits the significance of that noncompliance. The punishment should equal the crime. The chief executive officer uses the results of the institutional risk assessment to identify the significance of noncompliance in any area. Determination of the appropriateness of consequences is then made on an individual basis unless the institution has developed a mechanism of progressive consequences for noncompliance in each area identified by the risk assessment.

Lesson Learned

There is little guidance on establishing levels of consequence for noncompliance. Those areas of the institution that have a clearly developed and progressive system of consequences for the various noncompliance situations that they face can provide a good model for the CEO to follow in all compliance risk areas. Specifically, there are models in the medical billing risk area, intercollegiate athletics, and some research activities.

The Institute of Internal Auditors Research Foundation

Share What is Learned

The final step in the validation process is for the CEO to promote the sharing of what has been learned out of each instance of noncompliance. In the U.T. System, this sharing is being accomplished through risk area work groups established by the chief executive officer. The process provides a venue for sharing information on areas of potential exposure, results of noncompliance, best practices for mitigating noncompliance, and where to get answers to questions. Chapter 8 discusses in detail the U.T. System of sharing compliance information.

Role of the Chief Executive Officer in the Compliance Program

U.T. System Chancellor R.D. Burck used a simple analogy to succinctly describe the chief executive officer's role in an effective compliance program. He compared it to a magnificent, functional building.

- The building has an architect or designer. In the compliance program, it is the outside expert, hired or borrowed.
- The building has a firm foundation. The compliance program has an action plan.
- The building is constructed of superior materials. The superior materials in the compliance program are the employees of the organization.
- The building has a keystone that unifies all of the parts. The compliance program has a chief executive officer that unifies all of the parts.

The chief executive officer is the keystone of the compliance program.

CHAPTER 5
THE FIRST SIX MONTHS:
GETTING ORGANIZED

The need is recognized. The plan is prepared. The champion is on board. Now it is time to make things happen. Four extremely critical steps must be completed in the first six months of the compliance program's existence: (1) establish the compliance infrastructure, (2) train the infrastructure staff, (3) develop a standards of conduct guide and general compliance training plan, and (4) perform the initial risk assessment. Experience has taught that the methodology used to complete each of these tasks, and even the results of each task, can hinder or aid the future success of the compliance program. The first two steps are discussed in detail below. The development of the standards of conduct guide and general compliance training program and the initial risk assessment are discussed in Chapters 6 and 7 respectively.

Establishing the Compliance Infrastructure

The most significant decisions a chief executive officer will make regarding the compliance program, other than personal commitment, involve the appointment of a compliance officer and an institutional compliance committee. Acceptance of the program and participation in the program by all members of the institutional community are dramatically affected by these decisions.

Appoint the Compliance Officer

All guidelines for an acceptable institutional compliance program require that the compliance officer be a senior executive officer of the organization. This is interpreted to mean that the compliance officer should report directly to the chief executive officer.

The chief executive officer can designate one of the current senior executives as the compliance officer or establish a new senior executive management position of compliance officer. Before exploring the pros and cons of the two avenues for appointing the compliance officer, it may be appropriate to review the normal duties assigned to this position. Table 5 presents these responsibilities as three general areas of activity.

The Institute of Internal Auditors Research Foundation

Table 5
Duties of the Compliance Officer

- Make compliance a part of everyday activities at the institution.

- Oversee the various aspects of the compliance program to ensure that they are being performed as designed.

- Communicate with the chief executive officer and other officials information on the operation of the compliance program with emphasis on those instances of noncompliance that require executive action or have institution-wide impact.

The first area of responsibility for the compliance officer is to make compliance a part of everyday activities at the institution. This means compliance must become a personal issue for every member of the community. Members must see how noncompliance can affect them personally. To accomplish this the compliance officer directs the development of training tools and delivery mechanisms, reporting procedures, assurance processes, and communication avenues, including a confidential reporting mechanism for employees to use to report suspected instances of noncompliance. Another major task in this general area is the compliance officer's responsibility for the development of a risk-based plan for the institution. Items of lesser significance, though still important, are the development of a compliance manual and the organization of a compliance function.

The second area of responsibility is to monitor the various aspects of the compliance program to ensure that they are being performed as designed. This usually entails performing verification activities regarding (1) training, (2) control of compliance risk deemed significant to the institution in the risk-based plan, and (3) actions taken in instances of noncompliance. The compliance officer's responsibility in the monitoring area is complementary to the efforts of the internal auditing department and not instead of those efforts. (The issue of who provides what assurance services will be handled in Chapter 9.) This general area also includes the responsibility to conduct an annual self-assessment of the compliance program.

The third area of responsibility for the compliance officer is to communicate to the chief executive officer and other officials information on the operation of the compliance program, particularly those instances of noncompliance that require executive action. Other reportable items would include the risk-based plan, compliance committee meeting minutes, and the self-assessment report.

It is very clear from reviewing a brief description of compliance officer duties that this responsibility is significant and requires a considerable time commitment from the person appointed as the compliance officer. The chief executive should always remember this when considering whether or not to add these responsibilities to those of an executive already in the executive management ranks or to create a new executive position for the institutional compliance officer.

Choice of a current member of the executive staff as the compliance officer helps move the program forward immediately. In addition, it takes advantage of the networks already developed throughout the community by that officer. The two major disadvantages are (1) inability of the executive staff member to devote any substantial amount of time to the compliance job because of already assigned duties, and (2) the perception that the issue of compliance belongs only in the functional area of the official appointed as compliance officer.

Creating a new position for the compliance officer has two main advantages. First, a clear signal is sent by the chief executive officer that compliance is important. Second, it avoids labeling compliance as a less than full community effort. The most significant disadvantage is that it takes time to select the compliance officer, so the program is delayed or begins with a temporary leader. Both situations are detractions. There is a second important issue if the compliance officer is chosen from external candidates. That person must learn the culture of the institution as well as implement the compliance program.

Lesson Learned

Appointment of the chief business officer, the most experienced executive manager in the compliance area, as the compliance officer automatically makes the compliance program a business affairs (administrative affairs) program. Consequently, faculty and staff in the instruction and student services areas believe the compliance program does not apply to them. This significantly inhibits the implementation of the program. When this avenue is the only viable option for implementing the compliance program, the chief executive officer can insure the cooperation of instructional and student services areas of the institution by assigning the chief academic officer to support the compliance officer in the two areas mentioned. This should take the form of a formal assignment of responsibilities and duties, which produces active involvement by the chief academic official.

Appoint the Compliance Committee

The chief executive officer, with advice from the compliance officer, must now appoint an institutional compliance committee. The committee should be composed of those executives in the institution that have the authority to allocate resources to assist the program in achieving its goals. Members would normally come from the senior management team. The committee has two main duties. First, it provides guidance and direction for the program. Second, it follows up on instances of noncompliance to ensure that appropriate actions have been taken.

The compliance committee is to the compliance program what a board of regents is to the entire institution. The chief executive officer should chair this committee. The compliance officer serves as the committee's chief administrative officer. Resource staff should include legal counsel and the director of internal auditing.

This is a policy and disciplinary action committee that is not involved in the detailed compliance activities. It is an oversight committee that assists the compliance officer in carrying out those duties that the compliance officer cannot perform alone because they require line management authority. Consequently, this committee is usually small in size and deals with high-level issues in the compliance arena.

The compliance committee should meet at least quarterly. During the implementation phase of the compliance program, and whenever deemed necessary after that phase, the committee should meet on a more frequent basis, usually monthly.

The compliance committee may find it necessary to appoint a working committee that represents all of the constituencies of the institution to assist in such tasks as developing the risk-based plan, generating program awareness, and ensuring discussion and consideration of all viewpoints. This committee is composed of mid-level managers that represent the major risk areas of the institution and/or the major processes within the institution. It is a working committee and may be subdivided into ad hoc committees as the need arises.

Provide a Compliance Function

Every compliance officer needs a support staff to handle the detailed activities involved in a compliance program. The primary duties of this support staff are to assist in performing two of the three duties assigned to the compliance officer: training and monitoring. There are four scenarios that describe the range of compliance function structures. The two characteristics that describe these scenarios are the complexity of the compliance environment at the institution and the amount of time the compliance officer can devote to compliance duties. Figure 2 presents these four scenarios graphically.

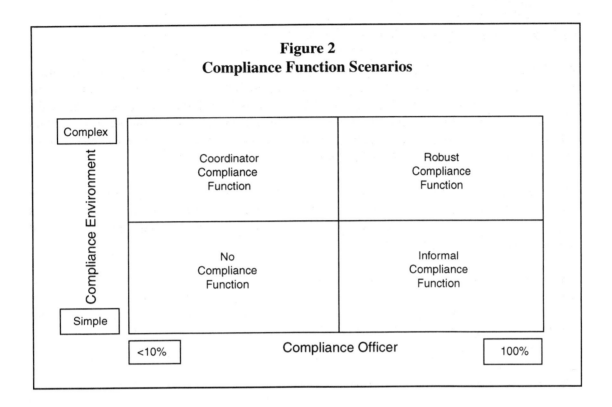

Figure 2
Compliance Function Scenarios

The "robust compliance function" exists when the institution has a complex compliance environment and a full-time compliance officer. A complex compliance environment may include research activities, intercollegiate athletics, on-campus housing for students, significant physical facilities, high reliance on information technology, and, perhaps, even hospital or other health-related activities. This is normally a formal organization with its own budget. The compliance officer's duties of training and monitoring are so extensive in this situation that a full-time compliance staff is needed to assist in carrying them out. The size of this staff depends upon the size of the institution, the resources available, and the risk tolerance of the chief executive officer and the governance function. (In The University of Texas System components, the compliance function staff size ranges from three to 15 employees.) In some components, compliance activities that were scattered throughout the institution, such as medical billing and environmental health and safety, have been absorbed into the new institutional compliance function.

At the other end of the scale is the institution with "no compliance function." The compliance environment is limited to six to 10 major issues, and the chief business officer is the compliance officer. In this environment, it is possible for the compliance officer to fulfill training and monitoring responsibilities using a certification process validated by internal audit and supplemented with external peer reviews conducted in the high-risk areas. (There is a full discussion of the certification and the peer review processes in the chapter on Assurance Methodologies.) This scenario works very well for small institutions that are engaged basically in undergraduate instruction with limited on-campus housing and activities.

The third scenario, represented by the upper left quadrant of Figure 2, appears to be effective where the compliance officer devotes little time to compliance even though the compliance environment of the institution is complex. This is called the "coordinator compliance function." Its defining characteristic is the designation, by the compliance officer, of a full-time employee to actually administer the compliance program. This approach is necessary when the chief executive officer is unwilling or unable to create a full-time compliance officer at the executive level. Therefore, to satisfy the requirement that the compliance officer is a member of executive management, the chief executive will appoint a current member of the executive team to that position. The compliance officer, recognizing the magnitude of the job, creates a compliance coordinator position dedicated 100 percent to the compliance program and delegates to that position the authority to carry out the training and monitoring duties of the compliance officer. The compliance coordinator can have a support staff of two to a dozen employees depending, once again, on the institution. The function is usually separately budgeted and has a formal organizational structure. This scenario works very well in medium size institutions that are primarily engaged in undergraduate instruction, but also have doctoral programs and some research. These institutions may also have intercollegiate athletics, on-campus housing, and community involvement. They would not have health-related activities, such as hospitals or medical schools.

Finally, there is the "informal compliance function" represented by a full-time compliance officer with no direct staff. This type of structure exists where the chief executive officer has decided to emphasize compliance by appointing a full-time compliance officer, even though the institution has a simple compliance environment. The compliance officer receives implementation and operation support from the institutional compliance committee, existing compliance functions, external reviews, and the internal auditing department. The only difference between this scenario and the "no compliance function" scenario is the presence of a full-time compliance officer. This scenario may be the most viable when the chief executive officer anticipates resistance and objections from the faculty. In that case appointing the chief business officer as the compliance officer would only increase the resistance. To eliminate that obstacle and increase the chance of program success, the chief executive officer might appoint a full-time compliance officer with whom the entire institutional community can relate.

Lesson Learned

When a compliance coordinator approach is used, the compliance coordinator is most effective when the person has previous assurance activity experience, such as internal auditing experience. The position of compliance coordinator deals mainly with training operations staff to assess and mitigate risks, and with monitoring to ensure mitigation plans are carried out properly. It is essential that the compliance coordinator understands the concepts of risk, control, and monitoring and is able to transfer that understanding to the people involved in operations in the risk areas.

Lesson Learned

The structure and size of the compliance function will vary from institution to institution. There is no best way for everyone. The chief executive officer must assess the culture of the institution and the magnitude of its compliance risks in determining which of the four scenarios to adopt.   Regardless of the scenario adopted, the compliance officer remains the responsible party for making compliance a part of everyday life, monitoring its execution, and reporting to the chief executive officer its activities and status. The compliance function is merely the tool the compliance officer uses to achieve those goals.

Training the Infrastructure Staff

Once the compliance officer, the members of the institutional compliance committee and any subcommittees, and the compliance function staff have been identified, they must be indoctrinated into institutional compliance. Many will already have some familiarity with specific compliance issues and processes. However, probably none of them will have familiarity with the concepts and processes of an *institutional compliance program.* Therefore, it is important that all of these players develop a common understanding of the program, its contents, and its expectations.

This can be accomplished in two ways. The institution can develop its own expert or experts, who can then train everyone else. Or, the institution can engage outsiders who are recognized experts in institutional compliance to perform the initial knowledge transfer. From the standpoint of costs and logistics, institutional staff appears to be the best choice. From the standpoint of acceptance of concepts and unfiltered presentation, the outside experts are the best choice.

This is not the time in your compliance program to go "cheap." This is the step that will provide all players with an unfiltered understanding of the compliance program, a common authoritative source for the program, and, really, the first impressions of the program. First impressions set the tone for all that follows. You can ruin or advance the compliance program with this one decision.

External experts come in several varieties. Both large and small consulting firms offer assistance in the compliance arena with expertise provided by employees who have previously been in compliance programs in the health-related arena. Another source of external assistance is colleagues from higher education institutions who are already engaged in the institutional compliance process. The main idea is to use outsiders. Somehow those within a community pay more attention to external experts than to internal experts, even when they say the same thing the same way.

Lesson Learned

Regardless of whether you use an internal expert or an external expert to train the initial cadre, make provision for continuous training patterned after this first effort. Compliance players come and go. Responsible parties change. Committee and subcommittee members change. Support staff come and go. There must be an ongoing process to ensure that all the players have a common body of knowledge about the compliance program. Failure to address this continuous training issue will slow the compliance process — and may even derail it.

Summary

While the chief executive officer is the keystone of your compliance program, the compliance infrastructure (compliance officer, compliance committee, and compliance function) is the foundation for an effective program. The initial efforts in this area are crucial to later success. This is said merely to introduce a lesson learned the hard way.

Lesson Learned

Start with what you have and build on it. As the chief executive officer attempts to launch this very important program, the following question may arise: Should I wait until I have just the right people and everything is organized optimally for success, or should I start with what I have and build on that? If you wait until you have a perfectly designed compliance program, you may be out of business. The experience of 16 U.T. System components as they addressed this issue has been to start with what you have and build on it. As a result, for some components the compliance officer and the internal auditing director are the same person and internal auditing is the compliance function, as well as the independent assurance function. There are others who began with the chief business officer as the compliance officer, assisted by a compliance coordinator who had no assurance services background. There are instances where the compliance function at a large, complex component was a full-time compliance officer only. Each of these situations represented the resources available when the program was started. They all achieved some level of success and some level of failure under their initial approach. The point is to start with what you have, but don't stick with that if it can be improved. As the three years of the U.T. System program unfolded, lessons were learned, some only very recently, which continually change the program. Those lessons are reflected in the information presented in this chapter regarding the compliance infrastructure and the training of the compliance players.

CHAPTER 6
THE STANDARDS OF CONDUCT GUIDE
(CODE OF CONDUCT)
AND GENERAL COMPLIANCE TRAINING

Development of a standards of conduct guide (The Guide), including a means of informing all employees about that guide, is one of the tasks that must be completed before the compliance program is "rolled out" to the institutional community. The Guide will become the standard of conduct guidance for all compliance issues that are relevant to the institution's stakeholders. There are three steps in this effort: (1) developing the standard of conduct guide, (2) developing the general compliance-training curriculum based upon The Guide and selecting the appropriate delivery methods for general compliance training, and (3) establishing a general compliance-training plan.

Kerry Kennedy, Executive Vice Chancellor for Business Affairs for The University of Texas System, Nancy Gast, Executive Director Institutional Compliance at The University of Texas Medical Branch at Galveston, and Carrie King, Chief Compliance Officer at The University of Texas M.D. Anderson Cancer Center, discussed the development of The Guide and the establishment of a general compliance-training curriculum for the U.T. System. In addition, they presented three different training delivery mechanisms. Their individual presentations are available on the conference Web site. This chapter deals with the tasks facing the compliance officer and compliance committee and the decisions they must make as they perform these tasks for their institution.

Developing the Standards of Conduct Guide

One of the essential elements of an effective compliance program presented in Chapter 2 is the establishment of compliance standards and procedures. The development of The Guide is the initial step in defining this essential element. The issues involved in its development may be defined by the following questions:

- What is the Standards of Conduct Guide?
- What should be included in The Guide?
- Who develops The Guide?

The Institute of Internal Auditors Research Foundation

Your institution's answer to each of these questions will have a dramatic impact on your ability to make the compliance program a part of the everyday life of the institution.

What is the Standards of Conduct Guide?

A code of conduct in many organizations is a policy statement by the management of the organization describing expectations of employee behavior and identifying the consequences of undesirable behavior. However, most institutions of higher education already have a myriad of policies and procedures in place defining acceptable employee behavior and consequences of unacceptable behavior for all areas of activity. That was the case at The University of Texas System as they attempted to develop a code of conduct. The creation of a new policy statement, a code of conduct, seemed to create redundancy, and its sidekick, ambiguity.

To avoid the confusion that a new policy statement would create, The University of Texas System decided to change the code of conduct document from a policy statement to an understandable summary of already existing policy statements. Their code would not create policy; it would merely restate it in capsule form. In recognition of this change of focus of the code of conduct, the U.T. System renamed their code of conduct. It became the *Standards of Conduct Guide* (The Guide), which is reproduced as Appendix H.

The Guide is a compilation of summaries of major policies affecting employee behavior. Each summary contains the pertinent information from the policy statement in plain English (and Spanish where appropriate), a resource person or department to contact for more detailed information, and the Web site where the specific policy being summarized can be found in its entirety.

Lesson Learned

Institutions of higher education should carefully consider the question of establishing new policy with a code of conduct or compiling existing policies in an understandable fashion as a standard of conduct guide. The compliance officer should seek the advice of the institution's legal counsel in making this decision. Besides the issues of duplication and conflict, there is the issue of acceptance of a new policy. Members of the institutional community are less resistant to the acceptance of a restatement of what they are already bound to do than they are to the acceptance of a new constraint upon their behavior.

What Should be Included in The Guide?

The Guide should include a summary of every compliance policy statement that is applicable to major segments of the institutional community. Included policies do not have to be applicable to all employees. Under this scenario, conflict of interest in research would be included in The Guide, even though it applies basically to faculty members. Sexual harassment would be included because it applies to all employees. Underage drinking, while applying to only a portion of the student members of the community, would be included. The exact content of such a guide is institution specific. Appendix H presents the model guide used by all components in the U.T. System and is an appropriate reference for any institution to use as it develops its own unique guide.

Who Develops The Guide?

The compliance officer (with the advice of the compliance committee) should appoint an ad hoc committee to develop the standards of conduct guide. This is a working committee and should be composed of representatives of all facets of institutional life. It is especially critical to have faculty and medical staff, if applicable, represented on the committee as these areas usually generate the most resistance to the compliance program.

The Guide development committee can become quite large if it is as inclusive as suggested above. To combat the inertia that attaches itself to such committees, the compliance officer may appoint several subcommittees with specific assignments. Areas of concentration for these subcommittees might be human resources, life safety, fiscal and contractual, faculty instruction and research, information, and federal compliance. Committee members would be assigned to these subcommittees based upon the segment of the institutional community they represent. In this way, the issues in The Guide that are most significant to each segment of the community will be developed by the representatives of that segment. It becomes the responsibility of each subcommittee member to insure that the specific segment they represent provides input, discussion, and buy-off on the elements of The Guide that affect them.

The compliance officer should also appoint one member or a small group of two or three members of the committee to actually draft The Guide from the information provided by each subcommittee. This editorial team will develop the overall tone of the document, ensure uniformity of presentation, and monitor for inclusion of all appropriate issues.

Lesson Learned

It is imperative that all major segments of the institutional community are represented on the development committee and on appropriate subcommittees. This is not enough, though. These representatives must continually inform their peers of the work of applicable subcommittees so that those to whom The Guide will apply are given an adequate opportunity to participate in dialogue and decisions. It is only through such inclusion that resistance to the compliance program can be met and overcome. This means that the faculty representative(s) should not be administrators who are also faculty members. There should be a representative(s) from the faculty senate and, perhaps, a faculty representative who is not in the faculty senate. Rank and file employees should have a representative. It is the compliance officer's responsibility to insure an appropriate representation on the committee and appropriate activity from all committee members. While this may be difficult to achieve, it will produce significant benefits during the implementation phase of the program.

Developing the General Compliance-training Curriculum and Selecting the Delivery Mechanism(s)

Another essential element of an acceptable and effective compliance program is to effectively communicate the standards and procedures to all employees. This process of communication to all employees is usually labeled "general compliance training." There are four major tasks in implementing a process that will satisfy the requirement for general compliance training. First, the curriculum for the training must be established. Second, appropriate content must be developed for each topic in the curriculum. Third, a method of testing the participant's understanding of the compliance program after completion of the training must be developed. Finally, a delivery mechanism or mechanisms must be chosen.

Establishing the Curriculum

The curriculum for general compliance training should be based upon the *Standards of Conduct Guide*. Those issues in The Guide that affect most of the institutional community should be included in the general compliance-training curriculum. Once again, there is no fixed set of issues that will apply to every institution of higher education. The subset of The Guide that becomes the general compliance-training curriculum depends upon the activities in the institution and the culture of the institution.

The most effective way to develop this curriculum is to establish a subcommittee of the ad hoc committee that develops The Guide. This subcommittee will determine what issues presented in The Guide apply to virtually all employees. That set of issues will then be presented to the compliance officer and the compliance committee for consideration as the curriculum for general compliance training. Table 6 is a summary of the General Compliance-training Curriculum adopted by The University of Texas System Compliance Program.

A comparison of Table 6 to Appendix H, the Standards of Conduct Guide, will illustrate the relationship between these two products.

Table 6 General Compliance-training Curriculum	
Area	**Activity**
Compliance Program	Mission Statement
	Goals and Objectives
	Program structure and personnel
	Confidential Reporting Mechanism
	Personal Responsibility for Compliance
	Consequences of Noncompliance
Regulatory & Oversight	Media Contact
	Government and Outside Investigators
Business & Patient Care	Confidentiality
	Accuracy, Retention, and Disposal of Records
Workplace Conduct	Conflict of Interest and Ethics
	Contracts and Agreements
	Drug and Weapon Free Workplace
	Copyright
	Privacy Act
	Health and Safety
	Use of Employer Owned Assets and Property
	Fraud
	Purchasing and Procurement
Employment	Background Checks and Criminal Offense Reporting
	Equal Employment Opportunities
	Sexual Harassment
	Family Medical Leave Act
	Fair Labor Standards Act
	Americans with Disabilities Act
	Gifts and Gratuities
Political Activities	Contributions
	Time
Environment	Hazardous Waste
	Hazardous Materials Awareness
	Resource Conservation & Recovery Act of 1976

Developing the Content for Each Topic in the Curriculum

The development of the content for each topic in the curriculum has significant impact on how the institutional community perceives the compliance program. In addition, the content of each topic may also have legal implications. Consequently, topic content development should proceed through a series of steps designed to insure accuracy of information presented, understandability of information presented, and recognition of legal ramifications of information presented. Successful accomplishment of these three tasks may appear incompatible. Nevertheless, they must be done.

Subject matter experts should initially develop the content for each topic in the general compliance-training curriculum. Their task is to ensure that the information presented on the topic is accurate, and that it is the most relevant information needed by employees to achieve expected behavior. Part of the content experts' task is to identify resource personnel or departments who can provide the employees with more detailed information on the topic. They should also provide in the content material the Web site address for the full text of the law, rule and regulation, or policy and procedure, which is the source of the topic.

Personnel trained in communication for understanding, such as training specialists and cultural diversity specialists, should review the content developed by the subject matter experts to ensure that it is presented so that the targeted employee population will understand it. Specifically, jargon and technical terms that most employees would not be familiar with should be eliminated. This task also involves ensuring that employee groups with different levels of educational background and/or with different primary language requirements will have a common understanding of the information being presented.

Finally, the institution's legal counsel should review the topic content developed by the first two groups to ensure that (1) new policy is not established, and (2) existing policy is correctly interpreted and abstracted. While this process may result in making the topic content less understandable (more legalese), it is absolutely necessary to minimize conflict in official, published information and to minimize the potential for litigation.

Lesson Learned

Review, review, review. Once all three groups (content experts, communication specialists, and legal counsel) have acted upon the topic content, it should be reviewed again by the content experts to ensure the accuracy of the information presented. In addition, once the content has been incorporated into the selected delivery mechanisms, such as video, interactive Web, printed material, or PowerPoint presentations, it should be reviewed by all three groups to ensure that it continues to represent accurate information presented in the most understandable language possible.

The Institute of Internal Auditors Research Foundation

This final review is necessary because the author of the particular training delivery mechanism may shorten or expand what was in the approved content in order to achieve the delivery impact desired. Failure to do this can subject the institution to the risk of litigation and increasing resistance to the compliance program on the part of some members of the institutional community.

Developing a Testing Methodology

Effectively communicating compliance program standards and procedures to all employees means providing them with the necessary information and ensuring that they understand what this information means to them in the performance of their assigned roles. So covering the right subjects and having the correct content for those subjects in the general compliance-training program is not enough. The institution must be able to demonstrate that the employees understood the information, which was presented to the employees. The only method that provides documentary evidence of this understanding is a test taken at the end of each training session.

To minimize negative reaction to the testing process, several key strategies should be incorporated in the testing process. These strategies are:

- Test at the end of each learning session, which could mean class period, Web module, workbook chapter, etc.
- Test for recognition of compliance-sensitive situations and where to go for guidance.
- Make the test short, no more than five questions for a 10- to 15-minute session and use that ratio for longer sessions.
- Provide for immediate assessment of the answer given and easy return to the appropriate section of the instructional material so that the test taker can refresh their memory and then re-answer the question.
- Provide immediate acknowledgement of successful completion, including a certificate if desired.
- Provide for documentation of completion in the general compliance-training database and notification of completion to the employee's supervisor.

The key is to test general perceptions related to the compliance program, not specific facts. Table 7 presents an example of test questions for one of the Web-based general compliance-training modules in the U.T. System compliance program.

Table 7
General Compliance-training Test Question Examples

Minimizing fraud, waste, and abuse is the responsibility of all employees of the institution?
True   False

If departmental internal controls are weak or poorly monitored, it increases the chance that fraud or errors could be overlooked.   True   False

Licensed computer software can be copied as many times as needed as long as it is for educational purposes.   True   False

During the training, references were provided on who to call and where to find more information if you have questions.   True   False

---

Lesson Learned

Design the questions so they may be used with any delivery mechanism. If possible, design the testing process to capture percentage of times a question is answered correctly on the first try. This provides an ability to evaluate each question from the standpoint of coverage in the instructional material, understandability of presentation, and other characteristics. Finally, use technology where possible in the taking, grading, and recording of the test for each employee. This last point becomes more important as the number of employees in the institution increases.

Choosing the Delivery Mechanism(s)

The general compliance-training curriculum has been adopted and the content for each topic in the curriculum has been appropriately developed. The question now is, "How do we deliver this information to our employees?" Choosing the delivery mechanism(s) involves two tasks. First, the total universe of people to be trained, which may include regular employees, part-time employees, and even students, must be analyzed to determine if a single delivery method will produce acceptable results. Second, based upon the output of task one, appropriate delivery mechanisms must be chosen for each identified group to be trained. A subcommittee of the ad hoc committee to develop the standards of conduct guide, appointed by the compliance officer, is usually charged with these tasks.

The first task, determining whether one delivery mechanism will work for all employees, is usually not difficult in higher education. The collegial environment has historically provided a natural division of employees into faculty and non-faculty categories. This fact alone will probably dictate multiple delivery mechanisms. In addition, though, these two groups can be divided into numerous homogeneous subgroups. There are many factors, exclusive of cost, which must be considered in choosing the delivery mechanisms for your institution. Table 8 summarizes the factors that should be considered. Each institution must determine which factors are significant in their environment.

Table 8
Factors for Deciding on Training Delivery Mechanisms

- Number of employees to be trained
- Availability of computers
- Technology of computers that are available
- Employee comfort with using computers
- Native languages in the workforce
- Ability to read
- Work schedules
- Responsiveness to various training delivery methods
- Instructional software already available
- Training tracking software already available
- Availability of software for purchase
- Time period for delivery of training

The second task is to choose the training delivery mechanism(s) that will produce the most effective knowledge transfer for your institution. Table 9 lists several of the most common training delivery mechanisms currently being used in compliance programs.

Table 9
Currently Used Training Delivery Mechanisms

- Face-to-face lecture
- Face-to-face interactive
- Face-to-face contest or game-playing
- Written workbooks
- Traveling poster board presentation
- Computer-based tutorial
- Web-based tutorial
- Web-based multimedia
- Web-based interactive

Typically, an institution will need to provide face-to-face training, some type of Web-based training, and, perhaps, written material for individual training. Web-based training is usually necessary to accommodate faculty, medical staff, shift workers, and others who find it difficult to attend face-to-face training or to effectively learn in that environment. Face-to-face training and printed materials are necessary to accommodate those employees without access to computers, those who are not computer literate, and those that have reading difficulties.

The task is not as simple as it sounds. There are many Web-based training tools, from the static visual PowerPoint slide presentation to streaming video with interactive capabilities. In addition, printed materials can take the form of storybook posters, individual workbooks, and master workbooks that must be checked out and returned. The spectrum of face-to-face presentations runs from a game-playing, interactive dialogue scenario to a lecture with or without visual aids. Consequently, the work of the subcommittee assigned to this task is to determine what combination of delivery approaches will produce the most significant impression upon the employees of the institution.

Several of the delivery mechanisms listed in Table 8 were presented in detail during the conference. Kerry Kennedy provided an overview of the face-to-face game playing, interactive dialogue mechanism, including the use of an outside facilitator. This process proved to be very effective for a small organization. Nancy Gast discussed the choice of a third-party, Web-based production and presentation system to address the needs of an institution with approximately 15,000 employees. Carrie King showcased the inclusion of general compliance training in the existing poster board education process utilized for all employee education at her institution. In addition, three Web-based training delivery systems were demonstrated during the breakout sessions. The University of Texas at Austin and The University of Texas Medical Branch at Galveston demonstrated commercial products that their institutions have selected as their primary delivery mechanism. The University of Texas Health Center at Tyler also demonstrated a Web-based training delivery system that their staff has developed and which is currently used by many of the U.T. System components.

Lesson Learned

There is no universal set of delivery mechanisms that will work for everyone. One component institution in the U.T. System uses a face-to-face delivery mechanism for all employees, including the faculty. The U.T. System has also discovered that as the number of employees to be trained increases, the options for delivering that training decrease. As an example, the two components with over 15,000 employees each find that only the most sophisticated Web-driven mechanisms can reach all employees with a consistent message in the time period required.

The optimal combination of delivery mechanisms depends upon the complexity of the institution, the number of employees, and the institutional culture. In addition, the initial mechanisms chosen may need to be reviewed and changed as the program matures. This is not only a function of the fact that employee knowledge and understanding change as the program matures, but is also a function of the improvements in the technology available for delivery of training.

Developing the General Compliance-training Plan

By now you should be thoroughly convinced of the complexity and magnitude of developing a standards of conduct guide and translating it into a general compliance-training program. In fact, the process includes so many tasks, and they are so dependent upon each other, that a General Compliance-training Action Plan should be developed. The plan should identify the responsible party and the due date for completion of each of the items in Table 10, General Compliance-training Action Plan Tasks.

The development phase tasks have already been dealt with in this chapter. Now, we will discuss the execution phase tasks and the administrative tasks in the table.

The Institute of Internal Auditors Research Foundation

Table 10
General Compliance-training Action Plan Tasks

Development Tasks
- Establish the General Compliance Training Curriculum
- Develop the content for each topic in the curriculum
- Develop the testing methodology
- Choose the delivery mechanism(s)
- Develop a record management system for training records

Execution Tasks
- Pilot project
- Initial training schedule for current employees
- Training schedule for new employees
- Planning schedule for the second and subsequent years

Administrative Tasks
- Establish measurable goals for general compliance training
- Maintain training records for all employees
- Provide mechanisms for reporting required training, completed training, and training not completed for employees, departments, and the institution
- Provide capability for all employees and supervisors to view appropriate records

---

Execution Phase Tasks

The execution phase should begin with a pilot training project. The purpose of the pilot project is to validate both the content and the delivery mechanism(s) of the program. The pilot project should include examples of all curriculum content that will be taught (including the same content for different audiences) and each delivery mechanism that will be used. Participants in the pilot project should be chosen to represent the various subgroups of employees identified earlier. Each participant, though, should complete all training included in the pilot project. This will allow the compliance function (1) to evaluate the need for separate content presentations for selected audiences, and (2) to evaluate the effectiveness and/or need for multiple delivery mechanisms.

In addition to the pilot project, the execution phase should include an initial training schedule for current employees. This schedule will detail when the general training will start, how employees will receive their training, and the date by which each employee should have completed the initial training. The schedule should also include information concerning status reports for the individual

The Institute of Internal Auditors Research Foundation

employee, for department supervisors, for the compliance function, and for general management. The schedule can be constructed to treat all employees alike or it may be designed around each category of employees identified earlier in the process.

A corollary task to development of an initial training schedule for current employees is the task of defining a training schedule for new employees. This training would normally be a part of the institution's orientation training for new employees. However, because of the amount of information that is provided new employees in such sessions, general compliance-training that is included may have to be in a very condensed form. When this is the case, the orientation training should be supplemented within a very short time period by some other delivery mechanism, such as Web-based training, so that the new employee receives at least the same amount of information on compliance as the current employee receives.

The final task in the execution stage is the schedule for training after the initial year. One might question the need to establish a schedule so far into the future. The rationale for doing it is to keep the need for continuing training on the "radar screen." An action plan step with responsible party and due date attached is a constant reminder that the issue must be addressed. So, to some degree, it does not matter how accurate the plan is for training after the initial period as much as the fact that there is a plan and you are continually reminded that it must be accomplished. There are two important considerations to remember about this future training. First, curriculum content must continually be revisited to ensure its accuracy and current applicability. Second, regardless of changes, the majority of the curriculum will be the same as last year, so plans need to include ways to vary presentation and emphasis so that participants are not subjected to identical information year after year. Both of these considerations have a long lead-time for completion. This is just another reason to schedule and begin addressing future years at the same time that you address the initial training.

Administration Tasks

The major administrative tasks in the general compliance-training action plan are to: establish goals for general compliance-training for the institution, maintain training records on each employee, and provide reports to individual employees, supervisors, the compliance function, and general management. Since a staff that is 100 percent trained is not a real possibility, the compliance officer (with the assistance of the compliance committee and compliance function) should establish a percent of total employees as a realistic target for the program. The U.T. System has found that a percentage trained between 85 percent and 95 percent of the total trainable universe of employees is realistic and acceptable depending upon the particular institution. The guidelines for effective compliance programs do not require 100 percent; they require an attempt to train 100 percent.

The Institute of Internal Auditors Research Foundation

The task of maintaining training records for all employees of the institution is far more challenging. The degree of challenge is directly proportional to the number of employees at the institution. As the number rises, the record keeping becomes burdensome. Consequently, decisions made concerning the delivery mechanism(s) to be used are usually influenced by the type of record keeping system that is or can be included within the mechanism. Many Web-based systems have internal administrative modules that perform the record keeping and reporting. This may be an overriding consideration in the selection of the delivery mechanism. However, there are successful systems that are homegrown. In addition, there are systems that gather information in paper form and input it to the electronic database through scanning or data entry. As the compliance function addresses this task, their primary record keeping requirements should be:

- Will it maintain an inventory of all content modules required for each individual employee and due dates when each must be completed?
- Will it automatically record the completion of Web-based and other online training?
- Does it have the capability to accept completion information from external media?
- Does it have the capability to record need for and completion of training other than general compliance training?

In the reporting task, the compliance function must be particularly sensitive to developing or procuring a record keeping system that is user friendly. The primary consideration in addressing this task is to provide a record keeping system that will produce reports of completion and non-completion of training by individual, department, division, and institution. Even more significant, these reports should be accessible by the appropriate person without intervention by the compliance function, information technology, or the vendor, if applicable. In other words, an employee should be able to produce a personal status report. A department supervisor should be able to produce reports on each member of the department and the department as a whole. The compliance function and senior management should be able to produce reports on the entire organization or any part of it. This accessibility to appropriate information is a key monitoring and motivational tool that invites individuals and managers to become an active part of compliance.

Summary

The ideas, information, and issues presented in this chapter represent the cumulative learning of 16 separate institutions over a three-year period as they attempt to provide effective general compliance training to employees numbering from 400 to 20,000 per institution. That learning includes the realization that we all have a tendency to forget about the planning process as we handle the day-to-day "doing" tasks of our job. In the case of the General Compliance-training Action Plan, this has resulted in duplication of effort, omission of significant tasks, doing before testing, and all of the other pitfalls that are experienced with every major project that is not thoughtfully planned. The timeline for a general compliance-training program, from the beginning of development of a standards of conduct guide (the basis of general compliance training) to the ongoing delivery of that training after the initial period, can cover two to five years. The U.T. System has recently discovered that some of the disparity between component institutions in the general compliance-training area has to do with failure to develop an action plan. As a result, current efforts are in place to provide all components with the information and processes necessary to prepare and execute such a plan. As that information is developed and shared throughout the U.T. System, it will also be made available to all institutions of higher education through the U.T. System Compliance Web site.

CHAPTER 7
RISK ASSESSMENT

The final step that must be completed within the first six months of the compliance program's existence is the initial risk assessment for the institution. Appendix E presents a simplified compliance risk profile for higher education. The primary purpose of this step is to identify those compliance issues that have significant impact at the institutional level. These are the areas that will receive the attention of the compliance officer and the entire compliance infrastructure. There is a secondary purpose, though, which is to identify all compliance issues at every level of the institutional organization and to determine at each level those issues that are significant for that level. Both purposes must be satisfied for the institutional compliance program to be effective. Failure to accomplish the secondary purpose will result in an incomplete risk inventory from which the ascending levels of the organization select the issues with highest institutional impact. The initial risk assessment, once completed, becomes the baseline for a continuous process of monitoring the risk environment of the institution. The final section of this chapter explores strategies for effective ongoing risk assessment.

Experience in the U.T. System indicates that complete information needed to correctly identify institutional high-impact issues is more likely to be available when the initial risk assessment process is a bottom-up process. The "best practice" initial risk assessment process described here will be a bottom-up process; however, alternate methodologies will also be presented for use by those institutions that are unable, for whatever reason, to sustain the bottom-up process.

Regardless of the methodology used, the initial risk assessment process should include the following tasks:

- Inventory the compliance risks in all functions (divisions, departments, work units), processes (basic research, human resources, fiscal management, instruction, clinical research, etc.), and activity areas (student affairs, development, legal, internal auditing, etc.) of the institution.
- Determine the significance of each risk to the function, process, or activity in terms of potential impact and probability of occurrence.
- Consolidate these prioritized risk inventories by homogeneous risk areas (human resources, medical billing, student financial aid, basic research, environmental health and safety, intercollegiate athletics, fiscal management, etc.), then review and/ or reprioritize the consolidated inventory to produce a prioritized list for each homogeneous risk area.

The Institute of Internal Auditors Research Foundation

- Determine those risks that can have the greatest impact upon the institution as a whole from the prioritized lists of each risk area, and define this group of risks to be the focus of the institutional compliance program (in the U.T. System they are known as the "A" list risks).
- Communicate this list of institutional compliance high-risk items to management.

The compliance officer, with the advice of the compliance committee, determines the methodology for the initial risk assessment. The selected methodology must fit the culture of the institution and recognize the existing skill sets and personnel available for the process. Three methodologies will be discussed. The bottom-up risk assessment process of completing the above tasks will be explored first. Second, the risk area subcommittee approach to the initial risk assessment will be presented. The final methodology presented will be the top-down risk assessment process.

The Bottom-up Initial Risk Assessment Methodology

The bottom-up methodology will be presented under the following headings: benefits, required conditions, work unit self-assessment, risk area consolidation, institutional "A" list determination, and communication to executive management and the governance function.

Benefits

The bottom-up initial risk assessment process has several key benefits that make its use especially advantageous. First, it immediately gives all of the employees of the institution ownership in the compliance program. Second, it provides each unit of the institution with the information to develop its own compliance program. Third, it minimizes the risk of institutional management failing to recognize a potentially high impact risk simply because it is not currently on their "radar screen."

Employee ownership means employee pride, employee participation, and employee group pressure to succeed. As you look for ways to communicate with the employees about the compliance program and to raise awareness of the program, the initial risk assessment process should not be ignored. There is no better way to defuse resistance and opposition than to include the potential problem employees in the actual process that they may be set to oppose. Those institutions that use the bottom-up approach find immediate recognition by most participating employees of the need for the compliance program and the applicability of the compliance program to them as individuals and to their work group.

Each unit that performs a risk assessment has the information necessary to become a miniature of the institutional compliance program. The unit can determine the compliance issues significant to its own success so it can concentrate resources where they make a difference. This little bit of lagniappe (something extra at little or no cost) can potentially be the most important benefit of the institutional compliance program. This is possible because it provides the vehicle for handling the large inventory of compliance risks that will never be high impact from an institutional perspective (known in the U.T. System as "B" list risks), but which still have the potential to negatively impact the institution if not properly managed. The compliance program infrastructure concentrates on managing the "A" list risks while the operating unit infrastructure (regular supervisory and operating controls) concentrates on managing the "B" list risks. The result — everything receives attention.

The chief executive officer, the compliance officer, and the compliance committee members are each concentrating on the issues that are currently impacting operations. "Out-of-sight, out-of-mind" is the axiom that must be guarded against at the senior management levels. This phenomenon might also be applied to the scenario in which these senior managers believe that a risk is controlled, and therefore, it does not deserve their attention and consideration. Both conditions actually occurred in the initial risk assessment process in U.T. System institutions that did not use a bottom-up process. For example, student underage drinking, not on executive management's "radar screen," and sexual harassment, considered by executive management to already be adequately controlled, did not appear on the top-down process initial "A" lists.

Required Conditions

Successful use of the bottom-up process for the initial risk assessment requires the existence of three conditions. First, supervisors and employees should at least be familiar with self-assessment workshop concepts and tools. While this discussion does not permit a detailed exploration of self-assessment workshops, information will be provided on their necessary ingredients and where additional help on the subject may be obtained. Second, the culture of the organization should be one of participation and empowerment. Employees and first-line supervisors must already be comfortable with sharing their knowledge concerning work processes, problem resolution, and continuous improvement. Third, the chief executive officer needs to make it clear to the executive and middle management team that time must be made available from normal day-to-day job tasks for the process to be performed. This first step of the initial risk assessment process could potentially involve from 1,000 to 5,000 man-hours, depending on the number of departments and the number of employees participating in each department. That is a serious resource commitment for any chief executive officer to make and must be weighed against the benefits discussed above. One final thought: ***Such a commitment of resources would send a powerful message to the institutional community about the importance of the compliance program to the chief executive officer.***

Absence of the first two conditions does not mean the bottom-up approach cannot be used. It does mean the compliance function will have to provide more training and support than it may have the skills or manpower to provide. Needed skills and manpower may be obtained from other groups in the institution, such as internal auditing, human resources, or academic departments. Absence of the final condition probably means that the bottom-up approach cannot be utilized in your institution. Recognizing that such a situation may exist, we have included in this chapter information on two alternative approaches that require a smaller commitment of institutional human resources. Of course, they also produce fewer benefits than the bottom-up approach, and as a result, may ultimately require a larger expenditure of resources to successfully implement the program.

Work Unit Self-assessment

The bottom-up initial risk assessment methodology is built upon each work unit of the institution performing a compliance risk self-assessment workshop. The term "work unit" may be defined differently at different institutions. Here it is defined to be the lowest level of budgeting within the organization. Any manager who has authority and is responsible for a budget is the head of a work unit. The purpose of the workshop is to assess the compliance risks that can affect the successful achievement of the work unit's goals and objectives. The workshop tasks are: (1) inventory all the compliance risks applicable to the unit, (2) determine the potential impact on the unit of an occurrence and the probability of an occurrence for each risk inventoried, and (3) prioritize the inventory into high risks (risks that need to be constantly managed), medium risks (risks that need to be monitored), and low risks (risk that can usually be accepted).

Self-assessment workshops are not spontaneous happenings. To be successful they must be carefully planned. The manager and staff selected by the manager plan the workshop. The objective of the workshop is predetermined: assessing the work unit's compliance risks. Planning decisions to be made include (1) the workshop participants, (2) the length of each workshop session, (3) how information will be recorded and by whom, (4) the methods to be used to identify, measure, and prioritize the risks, and (5) the development of a report to the compliance officer. There are as many successful workshop strategies as there are readers of this book. However, in the U.T. System, experience has shown that the following approach to self-assessment workshops produces the most useful results.

The optimal strategy for conducting a compliance risk self-assessment workshop (regardless of the organizational level of the participants) for each of the items mentioned above as planning considerations is presented below. Immediately following the optimal strategy, an alternate strategy is indicated in parentheses.

1. Who should participate in the workshop? Ideally, all employees in the work group should participate in the workshop. However, workshops have best results when attendance is limited to 12 to 15 participants. If this is the case, the participants should be chosen for knowledge of the activities performed by the work unit and should represent all functional groups within the work unit. (Direct reports to the manager)

2. How long should each workshop be? Workshop sessions should not exceed two (2) hours, even if that means holding multiple sessions to satisfy the objectives of the workshop. The need to attend to other assigned duties and span of attention are the two determining factors in this decision. (One 4-hour session)

3. How will workshop information be recorded and by whom? A recorder should enter workshop information directly on to a personal computer where it can be stored, manipulated, and reported. (Flip charts, blackboards, and post-it-notes can be used, but the information must ultimately be recorded electronically to be useful.) Each workshop should have a facilitator who keeps the workshop moving (but is not the workshop leader) and a recorder. Preferably these two individuals should not be participants in the workshop, as these other duties would hinder their ability to completely join in the workshop dialogue. Facilitators and recorders can come from the training department, human resources department, internal auditing department, or other areas. If the work group is apprehensive about having outsiders in their workshop, members of the work group who are not workshop participants can fill these two roles. (The work unit manager is the facilitator and the work unit administrative assistant is the recorder.)

4. What methods will be used to identify, measure, and prioritize the compliance risks? Identification can best be achieved through brainstorming. The facilitator asks each participant to offer one perceived risk until all participants have spoken once. The process is then repeated until there are no more offerings. The verbal presentation of possible risks stimulates participant thought and increases the probability of a complete risk inventory. Once the brainstorming has concluded, the participants should then discuss each risk identified to ensure that it stems from a compliance issue and that it is in fact a risk of this work unit. Participants may have in their possession an inventory of all the policies and procedures, rules and regulations,

and laws that they believe are applicable to their jobs. They can use these as an aid in the validation phase of identification. As a result of this discussion, items may be eliminated from the risk inventory. Items may also be added. (Accumulate all employees' lists of compliance risks in their jobs and produce an overall risk inventory for the work unit without discussion.)

Measurement involves deciding the probability of a risk becoming reality and, also, the impact of that risk, when it happens, on the achievement of work unit goals and objectives. Probability of the risk becoming reality is measured as *high, medium, and low*. Impact is also measured as *high, medium, and low*. The perceptions of the employees who perform the tasks that generate the risks are what are important here. Exactness is not needed, nor is it achievable. Identification of the relationship between the individual risks in a population of risks is the requirement. The high, medium, and low designations provide that relationship, and they require less time and detailed knowledge to ascertain. (Risk factors with values and weighting.)

Prioritization is simply ranking the risks based upon their combined measurement of probability of becoming reality and the impact that would have on the work unit. (Figure 3 is a representation of the risk measurement combinations.)

Figure 3
Risk Measurement Combinations

LIKELIHOOD	High	Medium	Low
IMPACT			
High	Extensive Risk Management Required	Considerable Risk Management Required	Manage & Monitor Risk
Medium	Manage & Monitor Risk	Manage & Monitor or only Monitor Risk	Monitor
Low	Monitor	Monitor or Accept Risk	Accept Risk

Extensive Risk Management = all LOCs & traditional in-depth audit
Considerable Risk Management = all LOCs & analytical internal auditing work
Manage and Monitor = all LOCs
Monitor = Operating Controls and Monitoring Controls from LOCs
Accept = no LOCs

All risks that have an *HH* measurement value would be placed at the top of the risks inventory, followed by *HM, HL, MH, MM, ML, LH, LM, LL* groups of risks in that order. If the work unit wanted to further refine the prioritization, they would address each measurement combination separately. As an example, the *HH* measurement combination list could be prioritized within itself by using the "pairs elimination" method. This means deciding on the most significant risk from that list and the least significant, placing these two appropriately on a new ranked *HH* list, and then removing these two from the unranked *HH* list. The process continues until all the items on the unranked *HH* list have been transferred to the ranked *HH* list. This is relatively easy to do if confined to each measurement combination. If it is attempted for the entire list of risks, it is unmanageable. (Prioritize the risk inventory by the numerical values assigned in the measurement phase.)

5. How will the results of the workshop be presented to the compliance officer? The Compliance Risk Assessment Matrix is a simple, direct way to report the results of the work unit's compliance risk assessment workshop to the compliance officer. (See Figure 4.)

Figure 4

Risk Assessment Matrix
(Name of Process or Function)

Objective/ Activity	Risk & Exposure	Potential Impact	Prob. Of Occur.	Rank Before Controls	Mitigation Strategy	BEST PRACTICES				Rank After Controls
						Operating Controls	Monitoring Controls	Oversight Controls	I/A Controls	
		H M L	H M L	H M L	Avoid Accept Transfer Control					H M L

The Institute of Internal Auditors Research Foundation

6. A single Risk Assessment Matrix would be completed for all identified risks that remain after the identification, measurement, and prioritization phase of the workshop. The matrix would present the prioritized list of work unit compliance risks. For each risk, the applicable law, rule or regulation, or policy and procedure would be shown in column one, the specific risk (and the exposure created if defined) would appear in column two. The third and fourth columns would contain the probability and impact measurement assigned to the risk, while the fifth column would indicate the measurement combination. Within measurement combinations (*HH, HM, etc.*) the position on the list indicates the ranking with the first item being of most significance and the last item being of least significance. Once again, this would be within each measurement combination. This methodology aids in the consolidation process by presenting all work unit results uniformly. Once the compliance officer and the compliance committee have identified those items of institutional importance — "A" list items — the individual work unit can then develop a plan to address the remaining items on their Compliance Risk Assessment Matrix. How work units can manage these "B" list risks is discussed in Chapter 12.

Additional information is available on self-assessments, including the workshop process, at The Institute of Internal Auditors' Web site www.theiia.org by searching for Control Self-assessment. In addition, there are aids for performing self-assessment workshops on The University of Texas System Audit Office's Web site www.utsystem.edu/AUD/resources.

Risk Area Consolidation

Risk area consolidation in the bottom-up approach involves reviewing all work unit risk matrices for those compliance risks with an *HH and HM* measurement combination. These are usually consolidated by risk area experts who are probably members of the compliance committee, if it is a large committee, or the compliance committee working group, if the compliance committee is composed of senior executives only. Examples of risk area experts would be the director of environmental health and safety, the chief fiscal officer, the director of human resources, the director of student financial aid, the athletic director, the manager of campus living, etc. The following process is used to narrow the task without ignoring unexpected sources. Each work unit's compliance risk assessment matrix is assigned to the risk area that covers most of the work unit's activities and, therefore, most of their compliance risks. As a control to avoid overlooking risks identified by other work units, each risk area expert will identify items on the work units' risks lists assigned to them (*HH and HM* measurement combinations only), which do not belong to their risk area. These "outliers" will be accumulated by the compliance officer and assigned to the risk area expert to whom they belong. In this way, a work unit that does not normally operate in a risk area can still provide information on compliance risk based upon their occasional or unintended exposure to that risk area.

The Institute of Internal Auditors Research Foundation

After the consolidated list is developed, it should be prioritized from the risk area perspective. The easiest way to accomplish this is to create a Risk Area Compliance Risk Assessment Matrix from the consolidated list. The first step in creating this matrix is to group the activities into homogeneous categories. The second step is to eliminate redundancy from the consolidated list of risks applicable to each homogeneous category. Then, the risk area expert and their supporting staff must go through the determination of probability and impact for the remaining risks just as described in the work unit self-assessment section above. The result will be a prioritized list by risk area that will probably contain risks with all of the measurement combinations, even though the input list of risks to this phase only included *HH and HM* measurement combinations. This should not cause concern because perspective has been broadened from work unit to risk area.

Institutional "A" List Determination

Each risk area expert presents their prioritized Compliance Risk Assessment Matrix to the full compliance committee or working group of the compliance committee for consideration in determining the institution's "A" list risks. This is normally a negotiation process in which risk area experts defend their risk area prioritization before the entire committee and advocate the inclusion (or exclusion) of items in the institution's "A" list of risks. Risks that currently have institutional impact are automatically placed on the "A" list. Risks that appear to have isolated or area-only impact are relegated to the "B" list. Most negotiation, dialogue, and outright argument in determining risks that deserve to be classified as "A" list risks centers around those risks that the institutional community believe are already well controlled and those that have not occurred at the institution and seem unlikely to occur. In some instances, the compliance committee or compliance committee working group may not be able to make a decision on a specific risk. When that happens, the compliance officer must make that decision, sometimes in consultation with the chief executive officer.

Lesson Learned

Never exclude a risk identified by the risk area expert as *HH or HM* from the institution's "A" list just because it has not occurred at the institution or because you think it will not occur. Remember the adage, "If it can happen, it will happen."

Lesson Learned

In developing the "A" risk list for your institution, treat every risk identified by the risk area expert as *HH and HM* as if there is currently no mitigation strategy in place to handle that risk. This is necessary for two very simple and time proven reasons. First, you may think and believe the risk is properly mitigated when in fact it is not. Second, the risk may have had and may now have an appropriate mitigation strategy that is operating as designed. However, there is no guarantee that this condition will continue to exist in the future.

Lesson Learned

Divide and conquer! (The "A" list of risks can contain from one to 60 or 70 individual risks. When the number exceeds 15 to 20, this list becomes unmanageable and leads to the belief that the institution will never be able to successfully mitigate any of these risks.) The solution is to stratify the "A" list into three categories. First, the critical "A" risks are those four to eight risks that are so significant they must be addressed this year. These are the ones on which the compliance function will bring all of its resources to bear, including assistance in assigning a responsible party, developing appropriate monitoring plans, developing specialized training plans, and actually training and assisting the operating staff in the risk area. Second, the well managed "A" list risks are those that you believe are currently being managed effectively. The compliance function will perform only oversight controls for these risks. The third category includes all "A" list risks not include in one of the first two categories. There will be very little compliance function activity around these risks. It is not that they are unimportant. It merely means that given the resources available in the compliance function and the risk area, these risks must wait until resources are available to properly address them. Please remember that use of this stratification strategy creates a new risk; the risk that something will happen in one of the tabled areas before resources are available. However, it is better to do some things well and some not at all than to inadequately address everything.

Communicate the "A" List Risks to Executive Management and the Governance Function

If executive management comprises the compliance committee and the compliance committee has played an active part in determining the "A" list risks, this step is unnecessary. However, in most cases, the executive management team has not been actively involved in the risk assessment process prior to this step. With that as the norm, it is imperative that the compliance officer formally presents the "A" list risks for the institution to executive management, including the chief executive officer. This can be achieved effectively by delivering in person a formal document. The point is not to just inform, but to inform and receive feedback. The compliance officer must receive chief executive officer approval of the "A" list risks for the institution. Now is the opportunity for the chief executive officer and any direct reports to challenge the list and cause revisions if necessary.

Finally, the chief executive officer and the compliance officer, jointly, should present the "A" list risks for the institution to the governance function. Ultimately, the governing board is responsible for compliance and the consequences of noncompliance. Therefore, since the "A" list is the roadmap for institutional efforts at minimizing noncompliance, they should formally accept or amend that list. This final step provides closure to the planning phase of an institutional compliance program.

Alternative Initial Risk Assessment Strategies

Risk Area Initial Risk Assessment Strategy

Those institutions that are not willing to commit manpower at the work unit level to the risk assessment process or whose culture would not support the bottom-up approach may choose to use the risk area strategy. This strategy utilizes subcommittees representing each risk area in the institution. The responsible manager for the risk area chairs each subcommittee. As an example, the environmental health and safety officer would chair the subcommittee dealing with life safety risks. The process involves fewer of the institution's employees and eliminates the consolidation by risk area step from the process. This strategy does not have the benefit of including a large part of the institutional community in ownership of the compliance program. In addition, it does not have the advantage of different perspectives on the various risk areas of the institution.

Top-down Initial Risk Assessment Strategy

Finally, there will be a small number of institutions that will want to use the top-down approach to the initial risk assessment process. This approach utilizes the perspective and experience of the executive and, perhaps, middle management teams to identify, measure, and prioritize the compliance risks facing the institution. This approach is useful in a "command and control" environment, when there are significant time constraints on the implementation of the compliance program, or when the chief executive officer is unwilling or unable to allocate any meaningful amount of resources to institutional compliance. If the latter condition is the case, experience dictates that the institution should not even implement a compliance program. Where the former two instances control, this is a viable although not preferred alternative. In the top-down approach to risk assessment, all the steps are eliminated except the final two steps — the determination of "A" list risks, and the communication of that list to the chief executive officer and the governance function.

The use of this approach interjects two very critical risks into the process. The first is that input from a limited group with similar perceptions of the institution can result in the omission of high impact risk items from the "A" list with the result that these risks are not managed. Second, failure to include as large a part of the institutional community as possible labels the compliance program as another of management's administrative requirements that has little connection with individual, personal job performance. Both of these risks can doom the compliance program.

Lesson Learned

Use the bottom-up risk assessment strategy. The alternate strategies may seem advantageous for quickly kicking off a compliance program, but the surcharge later on will be unbearable. Misdirected effort and employee resistance can cause the true cost of these alternatives to far exceed the initial investment in the bottom-up approach. However, if you simply cannot use the bottom-up strategy, opt for the risk area approach. Here you get some of the benefits of the bottom-up approach and fewer of the obstacles created in the top-down approach.

Effective Ongoing Risk Assessment

The initial risk assessment is only the beginning. Everyone from the compliance officer to the work unit participants in self-assessment workshops gives a sigh of relief, congratulates each other, and believes they are done with risk assessment. Nothing is further from the truth. In fact, they have just begun a process that will never be completed until the institution ceases to exist. Compliance risk assessment, in fact all types of risk assessment, is an ongoing process that must be carried out continuously if the institution is to expend its resources controlling the right mix of compliance risks at the appropriate time.

One thing we know for sure about risk — it is constantly changing. In fact, in the current higher education environment, it changes so rapidly that a mandate to perform risk assessments each year is worthless. Risks change more rapidly than that. Technology changes! The economy changes! Competition changes! The student body changes! Instructional delivery systems change! And none of these or any other area of institutional life change on a one-year cycle. The point is change happens every day and some of that change will affect your institution. So, the secret is not how often and when to update the compliance risk assessment. The secret is to constantly monitor the institution's risk environment for change and react to that change appropriately

The question, then, is how do you monitor the institution's compliance risk environment so that you are aware of the potential for changes as well as actual changes? There are three approaches. First, the institution can establish an office that monitors all of the institution's external risk environments — government, economy, funding sources, students, parents, employers, graduate schools, etc. Such an office, a chief risk manager's office, could provide assessments of the external compliance environment independent of the specific risk area experts at the institution. The second approach is to have monitoring mechanisms in place in each risk area of the institution. This has the advantage of being performed by staff who have the most knowledge in the area. It has the disadvantage of being performed by staff who perform conflicting duties. The third approach is to have a standing item on the compliance committee meeting agenda to discuss the external compliance environment and potential or actual changes in the institution's compliance risk universe. This method centralizes the process so that it is not ignored while still making use of the risk area experts and their staff to track specific sectors of the external risk environment. Regardless of the method used, the compliance officer and compliance function staff should continually peruse the various avenues of communication with regulators, benefactors, constituents, and others to maintain a pulse on the world in which the institution exists.

Adjustments in the institution's "A" list risks can be made at any time with the approval of the compliance committee, the compliance officer, and the chief executive officer. Of course, the governance function must also be informed. At least annually, these interim adjustments should be formalized and incorporated into an updated risk assessment that produces the next year's "A" list risks.

Lesson Learned

Don't get complacent; risk assessment is a continuous process. Risks that do not appear on your current risk assessment may become the most important risk issue at your institution. At various times and in various components of the U.T. Systems, such risks as underage drinking and sick building syndrome have made the "A" list without appearing on any underlying risk assessment list. Just because you developed a comprehensive, well-thought-out initial risk assessment does not mean you will successfully manage your compliance risk. This is a task that must be worked on constantly.

Summary

You are finally ready! Months of planning and development have taken place, thousands of man-hours have been expended on the compliance program, and you have not even begun implementation. In fact, most of the U.T. System components spent between one and two years preparing to implement the program. But now you are ready. General compliance training is being delivered to everyone. The risks that will require responsible parties, monitoring plans, and specialized training plans have been identified. The compliance function knows where they need to be active. In the next chapter, we examine the process used to manage each item on the institution's "A" list.

CHAPTER 8
MANAGING INSTITUTION
CRITICAL ("A") RISKS

Managing the institution critical risks was discussed in *The Effective Compliance Program Conference* by John W. Sparks, Physician in Chief and Medical Billing Compliance Officer at The University of Texas Health Science Center at Houston. His presentation and that of the staff from The University of Texas Medical Branch at Galveston demonstrated the maturity and comprehensiveness of critical risk management practices in the health-related arena. There are many examples of best practices in that area and there is a large common body of knowledge related to health-related compliance risk management. The Healthcare Compliance Association and others provide an active and informative forum for these issues. However, as is evident from the absence of presentations on managing non-health-related compliance risks, there is little in the way of information or published knowledge on managing compliance risk in a purely academic environment. Consequently, this discussion will concentrate exclusively on managing institution critical risks in the academic environment.

The "guts" of an institutional compliance program is the process utilized to manage the institution critical risks ("A" list risks). This risk management process consists of four elements: a responsible party, a monitoring plan, a specialized training plan, and a reporting plan. For the institutional compliance program to be effective, every "A" list risk must have a risk management plan that includes all four elements. The U.T. System compliance program has not achieved optimal effectiveness in its first three years of existence because of the failure to communicate clearly to program participants an understanding of this process. To remedy this situation, an extensive initiative has been inaugurated to establish a common body of knowledge for the institutional compliance program. The area of managing "A" list risks will be a primary recipient of benefits from this initiative. The information presented in this chapter reflects the common body of knowledge developed for each of the elements of the "A" list risk management process.

Responsible Party

Accountability is a consistent theme throughout effective institutional compliance programs. Accountability presumes exclusive responsibility. In the "A" list risk management process, accountability for managing each "A" list risk is delegated to a manager who is designated the "responsible party." An acceptable "responsible party" must exhibit each of the following characteristics: exclusive responsibility for managing the risk, appropriate knowledge to manage the risk, and necessary authority to manage the risk.

Exclusive Responsibility

There is only one "responsible party" for each "A" list risk. This is merely an extension of the management axiom that states "there can only be one boss." The purpose of exclusive responsibility is to ensure accountability. There must be no opportunity for passing the buck or pointing fingers. This is counter-cultural in many higher education environments. Consequently, designation of the "responsible party" for each "A" list risk requires chief executive officer (and direct reports) support and compliance officer insistence and perseverance. In deciding whom to designate as the one "responsible party," the compliance officer should constantly keep in mind that the person so designated must possess both of the other characteristics mentioned above; that is, appropriate knowledge and authority to manage the risk.

Lesson Learned

A risk can have only one responsible party — no exceptions. If the "responsible party" identification process for a risk seems to logically or inevitably produce more than one individual, one of two situations exists. The first situation could be that an "A" list risk is actually two or more separate risks. The specific risk should be reanalyzed by the compliance officer, compliance committee, and risk area expert to determine if, in fact, it is a combination of risks. If it is a combination of risks, the risks should be separated and assessed to determine if each is an "A" list risk. Based on this assessment, each risk should be appropriately handled. The second situation could be that one or more or all of the identified "responsible parties" lack appropriate knowledge or authority to manage. In reality, it is usually the authority to manage characteristic that is lacking. When this second situation exists, it is usually the result of the true "responsible party" wanting to avoid accountability for managing the risk. This situation is much more difficult to handle than the one of dividing an "A" list risk into multiple risks.

Experience indicates that some managers with both the knowledge and the authority to be the "responsible party" want to delegate responsibility, and therefore accountability, to a subordinate either on the basis of lack of time to devote to the program or lack of detailed knowledge about the risk being managed. There is nothing wrong with the "responsible party" for an "A" list risk delegating to subordinates the performance of activities to manage the risk. This happens all the time in the institution as a whole and in the compliance program. The chief business officer or chief academic officer who is the institution's compliance officer can delegate the day-to-day activities of the compliance program to a compliance coordinator, internal audit, or whomever they desire. The issue is not delegation of work. The issue is delegation of responsibility and accountability. The "responsible party" cannot delegate responsibility or accountability for the management of their assigned risk. The resolution of this situation usually requires chief executive officer support for the compliance officer's position.

Appropriate Knowledge to Manage the Risk

The "responsible party" must have an appropriate level of knowledge about the risk area to make decisions regarding the allocation of resources and the design of mitigation strategies to manage the risk. This does not imply that the "responsible party" has to know the detailed, day-to-day activities for managing the risk. Nor does it imply that the "responsible party" must personally perform the monitoring controls that are the primary mechanism for identifying instances or potential instances of noncompliance. Those particular tasks may be delegated to a representative of the "responsible party." That representative may be a manager who reports directly to the "responsible party" in the line management hierarchy or it may be a supervisor or lead staff member further down in the "responsible party's" line management chain. What the term "appropriate level of knowledge" does imply is that the "responsible party" has line management access to detailed knowledge relating to the risk being managed.

Necessary Authority to Manage the Risk

This is probably the defining factor in selecting a "responsible party" for any "A" list risk. The question that the compliance officer must ask is, "Does this position identified as the potential "responsible party" have the authority to allocate resources and take corrective actions to ensure effective management of the risk in question?" This is best illustrated by an example. An "A" list risk at many institutions in higher education is laboratory safety. Experience has indicated that the most likely candidate for "responsible party" for this "A" list risk is the safety officer of the institution. The rationale is that the safety officer is responsible for all life safety at the institution and has the knowledge to devise a plan for managing the risk of laboratory safety. This is evident because the safety office staff performs inspections of the laboratories to help ensure they are being operated safely. That is, they manage the laboratory safety risk. Consequently, the safety officer is designated as the "responsible party" for the laboratory safety risk.

An analysis of the laboratory safety risk is necessary to determine if this "responsible party" designation satisfies all three characteristics required of that position. First, we find that institution policy charges the dean of each college with responsibility and accountability for the proper and safe functioning of student laboratories. Second, we determine that the college dean, through the management chain of command in the college, has the appropriate knowledge to manage the laboratory safety risk. Third, we determine that the college dean has the authority to allocate resources and take corrective action to manage the laboratory safety risk. The only function played by the safety officer is to provide the mechanism for monitoring how well the college is managing the laboratory safety risk. The safety officer cannot correct problems with the application of approved risk management strategies. The dean can! The safety officer cannot impose sanctions for failure to manage the risk in the approved manner. The dean can! The safety officer cannot allocate

The Institute of Internal Auditors Research Foundation

more (or less) resources to managing laboratory safety. The dean can! Based upon this analysis, the dean of the college should be the "responsible party" for the "A" list risk — laboratory safety.

Lesson Learned

Designation of the responsible party for each risk is one of the most critical tasks in the compliance program. The compliance officer should walk through the above analysis in determining the appropriate "responsible party" for each risk on the "A" list. The result of this exercise will be the desired list of "responsible parties" for the institution. These are the players who will be the backbone of the compliance program. The compliance officer should share this information with the compliance committee, unless it was developed in conjunction with the compliance committee. Once the compliance officer and compliance committee are in agreement, the compliance officer should obtain the concurrence of the chief executive officer. This is an appropriate item to take to the chief executive officer if the institution has done a comprehensive and critical assessment of its most significant risks ("A" list risks). The chief executive officer has a vested interest in having the appropriate staff members designated as "responsible parties." Why? Because they are the chief executive officer's ongoing, everyday compliance assurance network.

Monitoring Plan

The designation of the "responsible party" signals the beginning of formal compliance activity in the "A" list risk. The initial job of the "responsible party" is the development of a monitoring plan for the risk. The term monitoring plan has meant different things to different compliance participants. Experimentation with several approaches to monitoring plans has produced the definition and process description presented here.

The monitoring plan for a risk has four sections. They are:

1. The operating controls that must be properly and consistently applied to manage the risk to an acceptable level.
2. A definition of the documentary evidence created to support application of the operating controls.
3. The supervisory controls (monitoring controls) that must be performed on the documentary evidence to obtain acceptable assurance that the operating controls are properly and consistently applied.
4. A definition of the documentary evidence created to support application of the supervisory controls.

Appendix I is an example of the monitoring plan for a potential "A" risk in the human resources area. In this example, the descriptive information on the risk appears at the top of the form. In the table, the columns are aligned to sequentially represent the four sections of the plan.

The "responsible party" (with assistance from a knowledgeable committee or staff member) must decide which of the many operating controls applicable to the risk are significant enough to require supervisory control review. There is no magic number here. It may be every control that is exercised or there may be only one or two operating controls that, if applied consistently and correctly, will mitigate the risk to an acceptable level. Of course, the optimal plan will have those controls that should produce the desired risk level, no more or no less. Choice of too many controls means utilization of resources without corresponding benefits. Choice of too few controls means a level of risk exposure that is higher than desired by the institution.

In the area of operating controls, there are many instances of documentary evidence. This is the area in which most policies and procedures in an institution operate. The secret with this section of the monitoring plan is to be sure the documentary evidence chosen will demonstrate that the control has been performed. Occasionally, we see monitoring plans in which the appropriate operating controls are defined, but the indicated documentary evidence does not provide assurance about the operating control. As an example, the operating control may be to provide each employee who will perform functions in the risk area with appropriate training. The documentary evidence is listed as the training curriculum and the notice to attendees of the date and time of the session. This evidence only tells the supervisor (monitoring control) that the course was suppose to cover certain items and was intended for particular staff. It will not provide assurance that the invited employees actually attended the course or that they learned anything from the course. More appropriate documentary evidence would have been a signed roster of attendees and results of testing to determine the understanding by attendees of the information presented.

Supervisory controls (monitoring controls) designed to optimally test the application of the operating controls are a required part of the monitoring plan. In fact, worldwide data indicates that the primary reason for ongoing noncompliance and unexpected noncompliance is the failure to perform supervisory controls. The supervisory controls in the monitoring plan must be specifically designed to demonstrate that the operating controls are being applied as intended. This does not imply the development of a new set of controls. Actually, most processes have an acceptable set of supervisory controls planned into the process. A knowledgeable "responsible party" should be able to easily identify existing supervisory controls that, if applied and documented, would suffice for this section of the monitoring plan. Appendix I contains some very good examples of supervisory controls that were already in existence and were merely incorporated into the plan.

The Institute of Internal Auditors Research Foundation

The final section of the monitoring plan is the identification of documentary evidence that the supervisory controls were performed. This is the area that appears hardest to establish for a monitoring plan. Many supervisory controls are performed without leaving a record of that performance. When this monitoring plan concept was being formalized, many supervisors believed that they would need more staff to perform the supervisory controls. However, they soon realized, almost unanimously, that current staff was already performing these actions. It became clear that the missing step was the documentation of those supervisory actions. That documentation can take the form of initials and date on existing documents or reports. It can also be notations written on reconciliations or exception reports indicating handling and clearing of problems. It does not require the generation of new documents or reports. Supervisory controls usually entail evaluation of information on existing documents and/or reports. The evidence of supervisory action appears on the same document and in the same place as the evidence of operating control application. The point is there must be a documented trail left by the supervisor that can be verified by an oversight reviewer representing line management, the compliance function, internal audit, or a peer review team.

Monitoring plans are not difficult to construct. The process is straightforward and understandable. Using the format of Appendix I, the "responsible party" can clearly document all actions necessary to mitigate the "A" list risk being addressed. An accumulation of all the monitoring plans will constitute the risk-based plan for controlling institution critical risk. That risk-based plan will become the criteria that is used by both the compliance function and internal auditing in providing assurance to senior management and the governance function on the mitigation of significant risks.

Lessons Learned

As "responsible parties" begin to develop their monitoring plans, they may need the assistance of compliance function and internal auditing staff who are knowledgeable in the development of risk and control models. It is especially important to have staff within the compliance function who have an assurance background. Those compliance functions that have former internal auditors, external auditors, and other assurance providers on their staff have been able to actively move their compliance program forward in the area of "A" list risk management faster than those that do not include this kind of staff experience. In reality, this may mean the diversion of some internal auditing staff into the compliance function for the initial period of operations.

Specialized Training Plan

The third step in managing a critical compliance risk (in fact any risk) is to develop a specialized training plan. This is an education plan for anyone who will be involved with the process that creates the risk. The specialized training plan will identify who is trained, level of knowledge transferred, frequency of training, provider of training, and method of knowledge transfer measurement. The foundation for the specialized training program is the detailed monitoring plan explained in the previous section.

Who Is Trained

This question may appear to have an obvious answer; however, it does not. There are three groups of institution employees who must receive specialized training. Each staff member who will perform one or more of the execution controls identified in the monitoring plan must be appropriately trained. In addition, every employee (supervisor or representative of a supervisor) who will perform one or more of the supervisory controls identified in the monitoring plan must receive the same training as the employees who perform the execution controls. Finally, each employee who will provide some level of assurance about the monitoring plan operation (compliance staff, internal auditing staff, peer-review team members) must be appropriately trained in both the execution controls and the supervisory controls. Figure 5, Specialized Training Plan Matrix, displays the relationship of each of these groups of affected employees with three other factors in the plan, level of knowledge, frequency of training, and provider of training.

Figure 5
Specialized Training Matrix

Who Is Trained	Level of Knowledge Transfer	Frequency of Training	Trainer Provider	Testing Methodology
Staff who perform execution controls	Detailed knowledge of control procedures	• New hires • Changes • Non-compliance	In-house staff	Test at end of training
Staff who perform supervisory controls	Detailed knowledge of policies & procedures	• New supervisor • Changes • Failure to apply these controls	External parties In-house oversight staff	Test for content at end of training Test for concepts through failure analysis
Compliance function staff, internal auditors, peer review teams	General knowledge of P&P; detail knowledge of control steps	• Prior to performing assurance services	In-house staff	Quality review process of assurance provider Organization

The Institute of Internal Auditors Research Foundation

Each "A" risk specialized training plan must specifically define each group that is to be trained.

Level of Knowledge Transferred

The level of knowledge that must be transferred to training participants depends upon the function that the participant will play in the risk management process. As Figure 5 shows, the employees who perform the execution controls will need detailed training in the process which includes those controls so that they not only understand how to perform the controls, but how those controls contribute to mitigating risk of noncompliance in the process. The employees performing supervisory controls need to understand the same things as those employees performing the execution controls. However, they must also receive information that will allow them to recognize the indicators that point to failures in the execution control system, including intentional failures (fraud). Finally, the assurance providers need training only in the specific steps required by the monitoring plan. They may also need training in execution and supervisory control information if they find that the monitoring plan is not functioning as intended. The specialized training plan must specify for each group of employees to be trained (as identified above) the specific information to be taught.

Frequency of Training

Execution controls training should be provided when (1) new employees are brought into the process operations, (2) there are changes in the process operating procedures, or (3) instances of noncompliance or potential noncompliance are identified. A refresher course for all current staff should also be provided annually. Supervisory control training should be provided when (1) new supervisors (or new supervisor representatives) are brought into the process, (2) new procedures are introduced into the process, or (3) absence of supervisory controls is detected by any assurance provider. All employees who are designated to provide supervisory controls for the risk should be reminded at least annually by the "responsible party" of their responsibilities through a refresher course. Finally, assurance providers should receive formal training any time the monitoring plan is altered. In addition, they should also review the appropriate training materials prior to the commencement of any assurance activity related to a compliance risk. As before, for each group of employees to be trained, the specialized training plan must specify when training will take place.

Training Providers

Specialized compliance training may be provided in-house by institution staff, by external oversight or sanctioning organizations, associations that represent particular "A" list risks, or commercial trainers.

•

The Institute of Internal Auditors Research Foundation

- In-house staff can be subject matter experts (risk area supervisor or "responsible party" or lead worker), training specialist, compliance function staff, or internal auditing staff. These trainers usually provide execution and supervisory control employees with information on the operating procedures required by the institution.

- External oversight or sanctioning organization refers to fund providers such as the U.S. Department of Education (an oversight organization) or rules enforcers such as the National Collegiate Athletic Association (NCAA) or the Southern Association of Colleges and Schools (SACS), which are sanctioning organizations. These organizations provide very specific and detailed instruction on the acceptable application of laws and rules and regulations that apply to the risk area. In the examples cited here, those risk areas would be Student Financial Aid, intercollegiate athletics, or instructional accreditation, respectively.

- Associations that represent particular "A" list risks are usually organizations of representatives from all of higher education or parts of higher education who are involved in a common area of operations. There are such organizations for physical plant directors, student financial aid officers, directors of research, athletic directors, police chiefs, and on and on. Many of these organizations provide training that supplements the information provided by external oversight or sanctioning organizations. The training provided by many of these organizations was developed to share experiences and apply collective knowledge to problem areas.

- Commercial trainers are those who provide training for training's sake. They have no other interest in the information presented. These would include the U.S.D.A, which provides training for many subjects not included in that agency's legislative mandate, as well as purely for-profit organizations, including the large CPA and consulting firms.

A combination of all or some of these providers will probably produce the optimal specialized training program. However, the actual mix to provide this optimal knowledge transfer will be different for every institution. It will depend on internal staff content knowledge and training ability, availability of association sponsored training, relationships with external oversight or sanctioning organizations, and finally, dollars available to spend on specialized compliance training. Specific "A" list risk areas have developed preferred training providers through years of experimentation. Human resources, environmental health and safety, and campus security come to mind most easily. Once again, Figure 5 provides a generalized template to use as a starting place for developing any specialized compliance training plan. The specialized training plan is not complete until a specific provider can be attached to each type of training required for each group of employees.

The Institute of Internal Auditors Research Foundation

Method of Knowledge Transfer Measurement

Every semester, month, week, or even day we measure knowledge transfer from instructor to student as we carry out the primary mission of an institution of higher education. It is done through test taking. We do that to determine if our teaching methods are encouraging understanding and retention of the material that must be taught. We may also measure whether the material being taught is the "right" material, that is, most current and most relevant to the needs of the real world. This is usually done through analysis of graduates' ability to obtain jobs in their field or to be accepted for graduate study.

A specialized training plan has the same need to measure knowledge transfer as the institution's general academic programs. The "responsible party," the compliance officer, and ultimately the chief executive officer need to know that each employee being trained is receiving the "right" training and that the training is actually being understood and retained by the employee. There are two techniques for fulfilling this need. The first is testing at the close of training, and the second is to identify and analyze failures in the application of execution controls and supervisory controls.

Both have their place in a specialized training plan. Testing at the close of training helps to determine if the delivery method for the training was appropriate for the group and the material. It does not measure understanding or retention of the knowledge transferred. Failure identification and analysis provides the best insight into whether or not the trainees understood the material presented and retained enough of the information presented to apply it correctly. The value of this measurement technique depends heavily upon the analysis part. There are numerous reasons for compliance failures in a process, including distraction, complacency, lack of understanding of knowledge transferred regarding proper actions, lack of retention of knowledge regarding proper actions, and intention to not comply. When using failure identification and analysis to measure the success of the specialized training plan, it is extremely important to determine the reason for noncompliance to avoid an inaccurate decision regarding future training.

What should a "responsible party" do about applying these two measures? First, the "responsible party" and the compliance officer, jointly, should decide which courses in the training program should have testing at the close of the course. This may depend upon confidence in the training provider and the provider's mechanisms to monitor the delivery mechanism, including the instructor. It may also depend upon the content of the course. Courses teaching specific actions in a process are more susceptible to this type of testing than those teaching concepts. Second, each monitoring plan should specify the analysis actions that must be performed each time a noncompliance instance is identified by monitoring plan activities, whether execution control steps or supervisory control steps.

The Institute of Internal Auditors Research Foundation

Lesson Learned

Knowing that there are instances of noncompliance is useless. Knowing why they happened is power. This allows for retraining of the employees involved, changing the process involved, or, when necessary, changing the employees involved. One of the essential requirements of an acceptable institutional compliance program is demonstration of a learning environment that minimizes repetitive noncompliance. That environment can exist only if the monitoring plans include mechanisms to ensure that training is achieving mitigation of noncompliance.

Reporting Plan

The fourth and final element of the risk management process for each "A" risk is a reporting plan. The reporting plan should include (1) activity to be reported, (2) what will be reported for each activity, (3) frequency of reporting for each activity, and (4) who receives the report for each activity. There are two types of activity that the "responsible party" should report. They are the supervisory control activities detailed in the monitoring plan and the training activity detailed in the training plan.

Supervisory control activities specified in the monitoring plan are the primary activity to be reported by the "responsible party." The information to be reported should include

- The number or percentage of execution events or transactions that were examined by the supervisory control, either overall or by execution employee.
  Example: The number of purchase contracts reviewed from the universe of all purchase contracts executed

- The number or percentage of execution events or transactions examined that failed the control attribute, either overall or by execution employee.
  Example: The number of purchase contracts examined that did not satisfy the requirement to utilize the competitive bidding process

- The identified causes of failure
  Example: Sole source procurement
        Buyer unfamiliar with requirements
        Personal preference of requestor

- The action taken, if appropriate, to mitigate repetitive failure
  Example: Provided training to all buyers
        Placed reprimand in file of requestor and provided training

The Institute of Internal Auditors Research Foundation

- The need for process improvement to mitigate repetitive failure
  Example: Computer program needs to require RFP # and Award Designation

- The need to escalate the consequence of noncompliance to mitigate repetitive noncompliance
  Example: Second instance for requestor; need to remove budget spending authority

This report on supervisory control activity should be made at least quarterly. However, if the "A" risk is very significant to institutional success, the report should be made monthly. The report should be made to the compliance officer. The compliance officer should share the information from the report(s) with the compliance committee quarterly.

This is not a report of specific instances of noncompliance. It is a report of monitoring plan activity and the results of that activity.

The report on execution of the specialized training plan should be a summary status report on the plan. The number of employees trained in each course in the plan in the current quarter and year-to-date should be reported. The report should be made quarterly to the compliance officer and can take the form of a copy of the specialized compliance training course schedule for the year with columns added for current quarter and year-to-date data. A detailed list of who attended each course is not necessary in the quarterly report. A mechanism must be available, though, to maintain such information. A simple solution is to include specialized compliance training in the same database that is utilized for tracking general compliance training.

Summary

Successful management of "A" risks requires:

- Designation of a "responsible party" who has exclusive responsibility for the risk, appropriate knowledge to manage the risk, and necessary authority to allocate resources to risk management activities.

- Development of a monitoring plan that specifies the execution controls that must be applied correctly and consistently to achieve the risk mitigation plan, a definition of the documentation that must be maintained of those actions, the specific supervisory controls that will be executed to ensure the execution controls were applied as designed, and the definition of documentation that must be maintained of those actions.

- Development of a specialized training plan that includes who will be trained, the training content for each target group, the training provider for each target group, and the measurement techniques that will be used.

- Development of a reporting plan that includes what activity will be reported, the details to be reported for each activity, the frequency of reporting for each activity, and to whom the reports will be directed.

This is the core of an effective compliance program. Here is where compliance or noncompliance becomes reality. Currently, this is the most misunderstood and misinterpreted element of a compliance program. The information presented in this chapter should provide a minimum standard for the process needed to manage an institution's critical "A" risks.

The Institute of Internal Auditors Research Foundation

CHAPTER 9
ASSURANCE STRATEGIES

One of the essential elements of an effective compliance program requires the existence of reasonable steps to monitor and audit for noncompliance. The monitoring phase of this requirement was discussed extensively in the previous chapter. The audit, that is assurance, phase will be dealt with in this chapter under the heading of assurance strategies. An assurance strategy is any process that increases the confidence level that executive management and the governance function have in both the reliability and relevance of the information they receive about compliance activities from the compliance officer. In Appendix L, The Assurance Continuum, this author presents both the ongoing and the periodic assurance strategies available internally to the institution. The ongoing strategies in the continuum titled Operating (Execution) Controls and Monitoring (Supervisory) Controls are incorporated into the monitoring plans discussed in the previous chapter. The ongoing strategy titled Oversight Controls and the periodic strategy titled Internal Audit Controls will be discussed in this chapter. An ongoing strategy not displayed in the Assurance Continuum but used in the U.T. System compliance program, certification, will also be presented. In addition, we will discuss assurance strategies provided from outside the institution, such as peer reviews and other external evaluations of institution activities.

The final session of the *Effective Compliance Systems Conference* included presentations on several of these strategies. David Larson, Vice President for Business Affairs and Compliance Officer at The University of Texas at San Antonio, explained the certification and inspection assurance strategies used in their compliance function. J. Michael Peppers, Director of Audit Services at The University of Texas Medical Branch at Galveston, discussed the two assurance strategies employed by the internal auditing function — agreed-upon procedures and audits. Sharron Devere, former Compliance Officer at The University of Texas Health Science Center at Houston, explored the use of peer reviews as an assurance service. Finally, Gayle Knight, Assistant Vice President for Institutional Compliance at The University of Texas Health Science Center at San Antonio, provided insight into the value of external reviews and audits as assurance strategies in the compliance program.

Certification

Certification is the assurance given by each manager or each responsible party that they are appropriately performing in their area of responsibility all operating and monitoring controls that are required. It is a self-assessment of adherence to established criteria for their operation. Usually, such a process would provide little value in elevating the confidence that the governance function

The Institute of Internal Auditors Research Foundation

and executive management would place in the regular operational reports coming from the same source. However, in the certification process, the manager is required to sign the self-assessment; in other words, to certify that what is being reported is indeed the facts. The signing of the certification is what provides increased value. Certification may be the only assurance strategy used for areas of operation that do not have a significant impact upon the mitigation of instances of non-compliance. The reliability of the certification process is greatly enhanced if either the compliance function or the internal auditing function selects a sample of certifications each period and verifies their accuracy.

Lessons Learned

Certification should be used for every operational unit, even if one or more of the additional assurance strategies will also be used. The certification assurance strategy has two primary benefits. First, it can be used to provide a level of assurance, no matter how small, on every functional area of institutional activity. This breadth of coverage cannot be achieved economically with any other assurance strategy. Second, it pushes managers to actually find out what is happening in their unit before they certify. This increases supervisory control effectiveness and it increases communication with operating personnel. Both of these are desired internal control features.

Oversight Controls: The Compliance Function Inspection

The compliance function exhibits all of the characteristics associated with oversight controls in the model depicted in Appendix L. The compliance function, including the compliance officer or coordinator, is a representative of executive management and is not involved in day-to-day operations. The assurance activities performed by the compliance function will take place within the current operating period. In addition, the compliance function will concentrate on verifying that the responsible parties performed their supervisory controls rather than on a review of detailed transactions. Okay, but what does this mean in plain language?

It simply means that the compliance function has a duty and a responsibility to validate the information it receives periodically from each "A" risk responsible party. The validation process is primarily intended to improve the confidence level of the compliance officer about the reliability and relevance of information that will be reported to executive management and the governance function. It may also, incidentally, increase the confidence level of executive management and the governance function. In fact, for "A" risks at the bottom end of the "A" list in significance, it may be all the assurance that is required.

The compliance function can obtain this assurance through an inspection process. The inspection process uses the monitoring plan and the specialized training plan as the criteria for activity in the risk area. Compliance function personnel will examine records maintained by the operating department(s) to determine that the supervisory controls specified in the monitoring plan have been performed and documented, and that, when needed, corrective actions have been documented and executed. They will examine individual transactions/events documentation to determine the proper application of operating (execution) controls only when they cannot find documentary evidence of the performance of supervisory controls. They will also examine specialized training records to determine that the specialized training plan was carried out.   Finally, the compliance function staff will ensure that instances of noncompliance observed in their review appear in a report to the compliance officer.

The results of a compliance function inspection are reported to the compliance officer and the compliance committee. The number of inspections that an "A" risk area has within a year will depend upon the importance of the area and the manpower available in the compliance function. Every "A" risk should be the subject of a compliance function inspection at least annually. This is not an audit as defined by standards regulating the services provided by either internal or external auditors. However, the compliance function can optimize staff effort and increase the usefulness of results by developing a work program for each inspection based upon the monitoring and specialized training plans of the particular "A" risk. The compliance function should also maintain sufficient documentation of performance of the work program to satisfy an assurance provider who is verifying the application of the oversight controls performed by the compliance function.

Lesson Learned

An acceptable inspection program requires the examination of documented evidence that the supervisory controls have been performed and that corrective action has been taken where appropriate. Simply talking to the responsible party about the information that they have submitted to the compliance officer does not constitute an inspection. Also, a verbal report from the responsible party to the compliance committee is not an oversight control. In both of these cases, the compliance function has no greater level of assurance that the responsible party is presenting facts than they had with the written report. For the compliance function to properly perform the oversight control, it must examine documented evidence.

Internal Audit Controls: Agreed-upon Procedures and Audits

The internal auditing function may perform three types of assurance strategies for the compliance program. The first is an assurance service for the compliance officer and is almost exactly like the inspection performed by the compliance function. The second is an assurance service for executive management and the governance function to validate the information provided by the compliance officer. The third is an assurance service for executive management and the governance function to validate the compliance program design.

Agreed-upon Procedures

When the compliance officer does not have a support staff, or when that staff is unable to perform the oversight controls in whole or in part, the compliance officer may contract with the internal auditing department to perform the oversight controls. The contract would describe the actual work to be done, hence the term "agreed-upon procedures." This is a contractual relationship between two parties. When this is the case, internal audit is working for the compliance function and not for executive management or the governance function. From an internal auditing professional perspective, this is a consulting service and the professional standards applicable to consulting services apply.

The process used by internal auditing when this relationship exists is the same process that the compliance function would use and is described in detail above. The internal auditing department reports results of this service only to the compliance officer and the compliance committee. In addition, any working papers should become the property of the compliance officer.

Lesson Learned

When internal auditing is performing the oversight function under contract or agreement with the compliance officer, the process is not an audit. It is not reported as an audit, and it does not have to comply with audit standards, although it must comply with the new consulting standards of the internal auditing profession. This is a two-party relationship between the compliance officer and the internal auditor. There is no third party to whom the internal auditor has a responsibility.

Internal Auditing Information Audit

The internal auditing function may perform an assurance service for executive management and the governance function related to information provided to them by the compliance officer. In this case, executive management and the governance function desire to improve their confidence level in the information provided them about the activities in the compliance program by the person responsible for the program, the compliance officer. In order to attain this increased confidence, they utilize the internal auditing function that is independent of the compliance program and therefore presumed to be objective in its evaluation of information provided by the program. This situation involves three parties — the group seeking assurance (executive management and the governance function), the group providing the information in question (the compliance program), and the assurance provider (internal auditing). This is an audit and is subject to the professional standards of the assurance provider, the internal auditor.

The criteria for measurement to be used by the internal auditor would continue to be the monitoring plan and the specialized training plan for the "A" risk. The specific audit program should be designed to ensure that the oversight controls were properly applied by the compliance function and that supervisory controls specified in the monitoring plan were applied and appropriately documented. Absence of evidence of proper application of oversight and/or monitoring controls could lead the internal auditor to expand the audit program to include validation of the proper and consistent application of operating (execution) controls. This would involve statistical sampling. However, if monitoring controls are properly applied and oversight controls have been performed, the internal auditor may limit any test of detailed transactions or events to a discovery sample rather than a statistically valid sample.

Working papers developed to support the results of this audit are the property of the internal auditing department. The reporting process for the audit report is through the normal internal audit process, usually to the audit committee of the board or an institutional internal audit committee.

Lesson Learned

If specific instances of noncompliance are identified during the execution of the audit program to validate activity information about the compliance program, the internal auditor should report those specific instances of noncompliance to the compliance officer and the compliance committee. The compliance officer will take appropriate action and report them to the chief executive officer through the compliance infrastructure. The internal auditor would also not include specific instances of noncompliance in the audit report.

Internal Auditing Design Audit

The internal auditing function may also be requested by executive management and the governance function to audit the design of the compliance program. In this type of audit, the internal auditor is concerned with the compliance process rather than the individual transactions. This is also a three-party engagement in which the assurance provider must be an objective party; thus the choice of internal auditing.

The criteria for this audit could be the document that initiated the compliance program. In the U.T. System case, it is the *Action Plan to Ensure Institutional Compliance*. If no formal plan has been adopted, the auditor could use the outline of an acceptable compliance program from the *Federal Sentencing Guidelines for Organizations* or from some other authoritative source. This audit may be a gap analysis between the planned compliance structure and the actual structure. It may also be a review of the planned structure to ensure that it is the optimal one for your institution. The internal auditor and executive management and the governance function should agree upon the purpose of the audit prior to commencement. The working papers belong to internal auditing. The report is issued by internal auditing in the normal audit report process.

External Subject Matter Expert Peer Review

An assurance strategy used by some of the component compliance programs within the U.T. System is the external subject matter expert peer review. In this case the compliance officer and compliance committee, sometimes with the advice of the internal auditing function, will engage a team of external subject matter experts to perform a review of the selected "A" risk area. The team members will be experts from a similar operation in a comparable institution. They may be recognized leaders in the field. This is a very attractive strategy in two situations. First, it provides a viable assurance strategy when the internal auditing function has limited staff resources. Second, it is useful when the internal auditing function does not have the specific knowledge to perform an audit of the "A" risk area. There is a third situation when this approach may provide superior results. That is when the institution is so small that institutional staff can carry out neither the oversight nor the internal audit controls.

External peer review members are usually reimbursed for expenses and are not paid a fee. Instead, the institution receiving the peer review services agrees to provide appropriate personnel on a reciprocal basis or to staff like review teams at the institution from which a team member comes. Occasionally, a peer review team member may not come from another institution of higher education and therefore may require remuneration rather than reciprocity.

The Institute of Internal Auditors Research Foundation

Most peer review teams range in size from two to five members. The complexity of the area being reviewed and the size of the institution are determining factors. Peer review team members enter into an agreement with the compliance officer as to criteria to be used, working papers to be maintained, and method and content of reporting. The peer review will take from one to three days. In most instances a preliminary report is verbally given before the team leaves the institution. If a formal report has been specified, it is usually available within two to three weeks.

There are several factors that will affect the value that executive management and the governance function will place upon the results of the peer review to raise confidence in what is reported to them by the compliance officer. The absence of presentation rules will adversely affect the value. The professional stature of the peer review team members will positively affect the value of the review. The diversity of experience relative to the area being reviewed will also positively affect the value of the review. Finally, the user's perception of the integrity of the compliance officer and the compliance committee will affect the value of the review. Regardless of the value questions surrounding the use of the external peer review, it has one irrefutable selling point. External peer reviews may be the only feasible way to obtain any kind of assurance on a significant risk management area.

Lesson Learned

The compliance officer and compliance committee should have a formal agreement with the peer review team that is signed by each team member. The agreement should address confidentiality of information obtained during the review, who will receive the report, how to transmit sensitive information, destruction of working notes, and any other item deemed important by the compliance officer, the compliance committee, or a team member.

Other External Evaluations of Institution Activities

There are increasing numbers of external parties that perform assurance services upon all or part of an institution's activities. They include federal agency audit and inspector general departments, state auditors, health care and academic accrediting organizations, and external auditors, acting as assurance providers or consultants. Each of these groups has its own purpose for performing assurance work on information generated by institutional activities. The compliance officer and committee, the internal auditor, executive management, and the governance function can all use the results of this external assurance work to complement the specific assurance work done in oversight controls, internal audit controls, and external peer reviews.

The Institute of Internal Auditors Research Foundation

Lesson Learned

Knowledge of all assurance activities undertaken by anyone on any aspect of institutional life could result in a reduction of control costs by eliminating redundant audits and elevating potential opportunities and hazards above the level of activity that may generate them. However, experience seems to indicate that much of this corroborating information is overlooked because its existence is unknown. A solution to the omission of such information from the decision-making process is to require that reports of all external evaluations of institution activities be filed with one particular institutional official, such as the general counsel, the internal auditor, the director of institutional research, or the chief risk officer. That official should also be charged with ensuring that information from these reports is distributed to all affected parties, including executive management and the governance function.

Summary

Table 11, The Assurance Strategy Matrix, provides an easy index to the various assurance strategies available for the compliance program.

Each strategy is defined by the following characteristics:

- Assurance service provided
- Assurance provider
- Information being validated
- User of assurance service results

The primary focus of assurance activities is to increase the confidence of decision-makers to an acceptable level at the lowest cost. Consequently, the specific combination of assurance strategies needed for each "A" risk at your institution is unique. It depends upon prior experience with information about the risk and its management, the significance of the risk to executive management and the governance function, and the availability of cost-effective assurance strategies. This is a decision for executive management and the governance function with the advice and recommendations of both the compliance officer and the internal auditor.

		Table 11	
		Assurance Strategies Matrix	
Assurance Strategy	**Provided by**	**Provided On**	**Provided For**
Certification	Responsible Party	Responsible Party	Compliance Officer
Inspection	Compliance Function	Responsible Party	Compliance Officer & Chief Executive Officer (CEO)
Agreed-upon Procedures	Internal Auditing	Responsible Party	Compliance Officer
Design Audit	Internal Auditing	Compliance Officer	CEO & Governance
Information Validation Audit	Internal Auditing	Responsible Party & Compliance Function	CEO & Governance
External Peer Review (in lieu of compliance oversight)	External peer review team of subject matter experts	Responsible Party	Compliance Officer
External Peer Review (in lieu of internal auditing information audit)	External peer review team of subject matter experts	Responsible Party & Compliance Function	CEO & Governance
External Peer Review (of the compliance program)	External peer review team	Compliance Officer, Compliance Function, and the Compliance Committee	CEO & Governance
Other External Assurance Providers	Accreditation Team External Auditors Regulators	Responsible Party	Compliance Officer, CEO, & Governance

The Institute of Internal Auditors Research Foundation

CHAPTER 10
NONCOMPLIANCE

The primary purpose for implementing a compliance program in any organization, including institutions of higher education, is to minimize the actual instances of noncompliance with external laws, rules and regulations, and internal policies and procedures. Chapters 2 through 9 of this book have presented specific steps that must be implemented to achieve that purpose. However, the proper design and execution of the various steps outlined in those chapters do not guarantee the elimination of noncompliance. So the question remains, "How does the organization deal with noncompliance?" The question has two answers. First, the policies and procedures that control the operations of each process utilized by the institution to accomplish its goals and objectives should include appropriate steps for identifying instances of noncompliance and an appropriate remediation process. Second, there must be a mechanism in place that any member of the institutional community can utilize to report suspected instances of noncompliance without fear of retaliation. In this chapter, we will examine the characteristics of both of these answers.

Process Policies and Procedures

In Chapter 8, Managing Institution Critical ("A") Risks, we learned that a monitoring plan is simply a clear definition of the execution controls and the supervisory controls in a process that must consistently operate as designed to minimize instances of noncompliance. This is the primary strategy of any institution for minimizing any compliance risk. The institution establishes internal policies and procedures to ensure compliance either with external constraints or with governance function constraints. These policies and procedures will be extremely effective in minimizing instances of noncompliance if they have two essential characteristics. The first characteristic has already been discussed, that is, consistent and correct application of these controls. The second characteristic that must be present and utilized for policies and procedures to be effective in minimizing instances of noncompliance is a prescribed set of consequences for noncompliance. It is this second characteristic that becomes the downfall of many institutional compliance programs.

Experience has shown that the development of adequate monitoring plans and the execution of those plans are attainable in nearly all institutions. Usually the proper execution of a monitoring plan is dependent upon a clear understanding of what is required and an oversight mechanism that ensures that what is required happens. Implementation of the steps described in Chapters 3 through 9 of this book should ensure that this characteristic is present and effective.

The Institute of Internal Auditors Research Foundation

Experience has also shown, though, that application of consequences when noncompliance is observed is nonexistent or sporadic unless there is a predefined set of consequences for the various types of noncompliance that can occur. The existence of this predefined set of consequences and the application of these consequences in cases of noncompliance is not a function of the compliance program of the institution. It is a function of the management structure of the institution and the management structure of the individual process. This is a fact that must be clearly understood by everyone in the institution.

To be more specific, operating policies and procedures that control activity within a process must specify what is not permitted and what will be done when failure to comply with the operating policies and procedures is identified. When an employee (administrative, staff, or faculty) is identified as operating outside the boundaries established by management, then the management that set the boundaries must impose the consequences. It follows then that consequences of noncompliance are not actions to be applied by the compliance officer or the compliance function; they are actions to be taken by operating management. The compliance officer, the compliance committee, and the compliance function are involved only from an oversight control standpoint. They are interested in determining if management has applied the predetermined consequences for instances of noncompliance of which they are aware.

One of the problems faced by all compliance programs is the apparent failure to apply consequences to identified instances of noncompliance. When this appears to be the case, a casual observer may conclude that management just doesn't have the "guts" to apply the appropriate consequence, or that the culture of the institution dictates "looking the other way" rather than applying the prescribed consequence. In fact, either or both of these may be the case. However, it is equally likely that management of the institution and/or of the process has not established a predefined set of consequences for the various possible instances of noncompliance that can occur. When there is no predefined set of consequences, management avoids applying any consequence because it will appear to be selective and not universal. The result of all three situations is the same. Instances of noncompliance will not be minimized because there is no personal consequence for the employee who breaks the rules. This is a death sentence for any compliance program.

What is the responsibility of the compliance officer, the compliance committee, and the compliance program when any of the three situations in the preceding paragraph exists? For the first two situations, the compliance officer (with the advice of the compliance committee) should inform the chief executive officer that the compliance program cannot achieve its goal of minimizing instances of noncompliance because of the organizational culture. Correction of this impediment to success requires intervention by the chief executive officer and the board to change the culture. If the third situation exists, the compliance officer should inform management of the affected process and the chief executive officer that the process policies and procedures need to be revised to include a predefined set of consequences for specific instances of noncompliance. The rationale for doing this is so that everyone involved in the process knows beforehand what the results of specific acts of noncompliance will be. It is then possible for process management and executive management to apply those consequences, when warranted, without incurring the risk of appearing arbitrary.

Lesson Learned

Operating staff and management are responsible for documented corrective action in response to instances of noncompliance (one of the essential elements of an effective compliance program as described in the *Federal Sentencing Guidelines for Organizations*). Such actions are remedial steps applied to individuals or design corrections applied to processes to prevent recurrence of the instance of noncompliance. Demonstrating the existence of this element in your compliance program may be the most difficult task you undertake. The solution to this problem may be to require a "Consequences of Noncompliance Plan" as a part of the package of plans that must be produced by the responsible party for each "A" risk. A better solution would be to require management responsible for each process utilized by the institution to develop a predefined set of consequences for instances of noncompliance with the policies and procedures applicable to the process. Table 12, Predefined Consequences of Noncompliance, is an example of this concept.

If these consequences already exist in the process policies and procedures, but are scattered throughout and therefore not visible, they should be accumulated for visibility and easy reference.

The responsibility of defining consequences of noncompliance and for applying those consequences rests with line management, from the first line manager to the chief executive officer. Actions to achieve compliance, identification of noncompliance, and actions taken to prevent reoccurrence of noncompliance are all the responsibility of operating staff and management. The compliance program through the compliance officer, the compliance committee, and the compliance function educates operating staff and management, facilitates the compliance-related activities of operating staff and management, and monitors the compliance-related activities of operating staff and management. They do this to provide objective information to the chief executive officer and the governance function on how operating staff and management are carrying out their responsibility to minimize noncompliance.

Table 12 Examples of Predefined Consequences of Noncompliance	
Identified Noncompliance	**Consequence of Instance of Noncompliance**
Expenditures for Unallowable Costs on Research Grant • First Instance • Second Instance • Third Instance • Fourth Instance	• Training • Reprimand in file by VP Research • Loss of Spending Authority • Loss of Principal Investigator Status
Failure of Drug Testing • First Instance • Second Instance • Third Instance	• Warning and Training • Suspended for Particular Event • Removed from Athletic Program
Intentional False Information on Application for Employment • First Instance	• Termination

Confidential Reporting Mechanisms

Another characteristic of an acceptable institutional compliance program presented in Chapter 2 is a method of reporting suspected instances of noncompliance which will shield the reporting party from retaliatory actions. This is usually referred to as a "confidential reporting mechanism." The purpose of the confidential reporting mechanism is to provide a vehicle for identifying noncompliance that is not dependent upon management. Thus, if for some reason operating management is not diligent in identifying noncompliance or is reluctant to take action on noncompliance, there is a backup mechanism that employees can use to bring potential instances of noncompliance to the attention of senior management and the governance function.

There are three issues that must be considered in establishing the confidential reporting mechanism. First, the site for receiving confidential reports of potential noncompliance must be chosen. Second, the actual process for handling all instances received by the confidential reporting site must be defined. Third, the specific relationship between the official confidential reporting site and other problem reporting sites must be established.

Confidential Reporting Site

A confidential reporting site can be any physical site that allows the reporting party to conceal their identity. It can be a special telephone number, a post office box, a drop box, or a particular office. It may be a part of the institutional structure, such as a telephone number within the institution, or it may be separate from the institution, such as a telephone number operated by an external party. The decision belongs to the chief executive officer of the institution with the advice and counsel of the compliance officer and the compliance committee.

When establishing the confidential reporting site, the primary consideration should be the level of confidence that the reporting party will have about their anonymity. In reality, reporting parties have greater confidence that their identity will remain unknown when they are filing their report of suspected noncompliance at a site external to the institutional structure. This heightened sense of maintaining anonymity should mean the normal person would readily report suspected noncompliance. Consequently, telephone numbers answered by parties whose only connection to the institution is contractual and post office boxes that are not on campus are usually more effective as confidential reporting sites than those on campus. There are independent organizations that will provide either a telephone site or a post office box site for a fee. The range of services provided by these vendors goes from merely recording a telephone message or receiving a written message to actually engaging the reporting party in a transfer of information necessary to investigate the reported condition.

Triage Process: How to Handle Reports of Potential Noncompliance

The second step in establishing a confidential reporting mechanism is to determine who will handle the reports of potential noncompliance and how they will handle them. This has become known as the "triage process" because of the need to immediately manage a situation that could be life threatening to the institution.

It is unacceptable to assign, either formally or by default, the handling of reported situations to a single individual. There are two main reasons for this proscription. First, an individual probably would not have all of the skills needed to properly address every reported situation. Second, and more important, if the reported situation involved the person responsible for handling reports of suspected noncompliance, that person could choose to do nothing about the report in order to protect himself or herself.

The acceptable solution of who receives reports to the confidential reporting site is to appoint a team of at least three senior-level managers to act as the review group for all reported situations. While the composition of that team may vary, they would usually be chosen from the following group of senior managers: the compliance officer, the director of internal auditing, the legal counsel, the director of human resources, the chief of research, the provost, the chief business officer, and so forth.

The compliance officer (with the advice and counsel of the compliance committee) should specify the process used by the triage team. That process should include the following steps:

1. Receiving and recording all reported situations, whether directly from the confidential reporting site or through other process's reporting sites.
2. Classification of reported situation into compliance-related and other.
3. Distribution of reported situations that are not compliance-related to the appropriate organizational unit; for example, working conditions, preferential treatment by supervisor, salary and benefit issues, and access to facilities issues.
4. Review of compliance-related situations and designation of what organizational unit or what employee will investigate the allegations and report back to the triage team.
5. Defining when it is appropriate for the triage team to personally investigate a potential noncompliance situation.
6. Tracking of received and recorded reports to record final disposition so that the anonymous reporting party can find out about the status of their report.
7. Reporting to the compliance officer and the compliance committee on the activity of the confidential reporting mechanism, including final disposition or lack of final disposition of every situation.

Generally speaking, the triage team is a clearinghouse for reports received by the confidential reporting mechanism, regardless of whether the report comes to the confidential reporting site directly or through another process's reporting site. They usually do not maintain detailed investigative and fact records of their own; those belong to the investigating organizational unit. The investigating unit will report back to the triage team with the results of its work and actions taken, but all of the detailed evidence supporting that work and those actions will remain with the investigating organizational unit. The results of the investigative work and the actions taken will be recorded in the triage team records so that their tracking system can identify open items, provide final resolution to anonymous reporters, and provide activity data to the compliance program structure.

Relationship between the Confidential Reporting Site and Other Problem Reporting Sites

The institutional compliance program is a "late comer" in the organizational structure of most institutions of higher education. This means that most institutions already have well-defined and used avenues for reporting situations that an employee may feel violate institution policies and procedures or federal, state, or local laws and rules and regulations. Examples of these avenues for reporting are found in the processes of human resources, fiscal accountability, research integrity, and institutional ethics. Some reporting parties may elect to report their suspected noncompliance through one of these existing channels, rather than to the compliance confidential reporting site.

The compliance officer (with the advice of the compliance committee) should establish the process for receiving true noncompliance allegations from these other problem reporting and resolution sites. This process should at a minimum address the following questions:

- Which reports received by other reporting sites should be forwarded to the compliance confidential reporting process? All reports that allege a violation of internal policies and procedures or external laws and rules and regulations should be forwarded to the compliance confidential reporting mechanism.

- What information should be forwarded? All the information gathered by the initial reporting site, except the information that would identify the reporting party, should be forwarded.

- Who in the compliance structure receives the report? The triage team within the compliance structure would receive the information transferred from other reporting sites.

- What is the other site's responsibility after the report is forwarded to the compliance site? The other reporting site's responsibility ends with transfer to the compliance triage team. The other reporting site should record that they have transferred the report to the triage team so that the reporting party can be so informed if they inquire.

- What is the triage team's responsibility for action on reports transferred from other reporting sites? In addition to the same responsibilities they have for reports received at the confidential reporting site, the triage team is also responsible for informing the original reporting site of the final disposition on the reported situation. This allows the original reporting site to provide the most complete information directly to the reporting party.

Summary

A well-designed confidential reporting mechanism in the compliance structure will provide all institutional community members with assurance that when standard control processes do not appear to be working, they have another avenue to bring potential noncompliance to management's attention without fear of reprisal. A well-designed confidential reporting mechanism in the compliance structure will provide the institution's governance function and senior management with the assurance that when the normal controls are not working as planned, responsible institution stakeholders have another internal avenue for exposing potential noncompliance. This additional internal avenue, when properly managed and utilized, can minimize exposure to negative publicity, lawsuits, and regulatory actions.

Identification of instances of noncompliance is the responsibility of management within each process in the institution. The application of consequences for noncompliance is also the responsibility of management of each process. When either identification or remedial action does not take place within the process itself, concerned employees and other stakeholders can utilize the confidential reporting mechanism to bring such situations to the attention of senior management and the governance function. Those are the two internal mechanisms available to address noncompliance. The responsibility of the compliance program at an institution is to provide senior management and the governance function with ongoing (everyday and continuous) assurance that these two processes are properly designed and are being consistently applied. This ongoing assurance is needed because failure of both these mechanisms usually means the institution will suffer external consequences.

The Institute of Internal Auditors Research Foundation

Lesson Learned

Confidential reporting mechanisms are important components of the institutional compliance structure; but they should not and cannot be the primary mechanism for discovering and correcting noncompliance. The primary mechanism is the management of the operating processes of the institution. Adequate monitoring plans and specialized training plans are prerequisites to effective management of a process. However, they will never minimize noncompliance unless the process also has a predefined set of consequences that are applied when noncompliance is identified. This is the primary defense that an institution has against noncompliance. So, the message on minimizing noncompliance is:

- Ensure that every process at your institution has a prescribed set of consequences for noncompliance.
- Ensure that every employee who is involved in the process (administrator, faculty, or staff) knows these consequences.
- Ensure that any employee (administrator, faculty, or staff) suffers the prescribed consequence whenever they fail to comply
- Establish a confidential reporting mechanism.

The Institute of Internal Auditors Research Foundation

CHAPTER 11
MANAGING ALL "A" RISKS

While institution critical compliance risks, "A" risks, are the object of the institutional compliance program's effort, they are only a small portion of the total universe of compliance risks faced by the institution. So the question can be asked, "What happens to those identified compliance risks that are not designated as institution "A" risks?" We will approach the answer to that question by first assuming that a risk assessment methodology other than top-down was used.   When the bottom-up approach is used, every level of the organization independently identifies its "A" risks and other risks. That means the work unit level and the risk area level each has a set of "A" risks that they need to manage. In fact, they each need to manage those risks in the same way the institutional compliance program manages the institution's "A" risks using the same process de-fined in Chapter 8, Managing Institution Critical ("A") Risks.

So that there is no question about what is required to manage an "A" risk at the work unit and risk area level, let's reiterate the requirements from Chapter 8. For any organizational level of the institution, the requirements for properly managing its "A" risks are:

1. Assign a single responsible party.
2. Develop and implement an appropriate monitoring plan.
3. Develop and implement a specialized training plan.
4. Develop and implement a reporting plan.
5. Ensure that there is a predetermined set of consequences for noncompliance with the detailed controls in the monitoring plan. (This requirement is not in Chapter 8, but comes from Chapter 10, Noncompliance).

The process is the same at every level of activity in the institution.

The only difference then in managing the "A" risks at the institution level and at the risk area or work unit level is who provides the oversight control function. Table 13, Oversight Controls for "A" Risks at All Levels of the Institution, summarizes this difference.

The "A" risks of each work unit (the lowest organizational level) are passed up to the appropriate risk area (intermediate organizational level). Here they are combined with risks that exist specifi-cally at the risk area level to obtain the risk universe for the risk area. The risk area then prioritizes this universe into the risk area "A" risks and "B" risks. Each risk area's "A" risks are passed up to the institution level and combined with risks specific to the institution as a whole to become that institution's risk universe.

The Institute of Internal Auditors Research Foundation

Table 13
Oversight Controls for "A" Risks at All Levels of the Institution

Institutional Level	"A" Risks Covered	Who Provides Oversight Controls	On Whom Oversight is Provided	For Whom Oversight is Provided
Institution	Institution "A" Risks	Compliance Officer and Function	Responsible Party	Chief Executive Officer
Risk Area	Risk Area "A" Risks not included above	Risk Area Responsible Party	Work Unit Management	Compliance Officer
Work Unit	Work Unit Risks not included in either above	Work Unit Management	Work Unit Employees	Risk Area Responsible Party

In this process, many of the "A" risks passed up from lower organizational levels do not become "A" risks of the organizational level to which they are passed. The oversight control of these risks remains the responsibility of the organizational level that first identified them. Thus, work unit "A" risks that were not identified as significant for the risk area (are returned to the work unit manager for application of oversight controls. The work unit manager then has the same responsibility for providing assurance of mitigation of noncompliance for these "A" risks as the compliance officer has for the institution's "A" risks.

In the same way, the institutional compliance officer and compliance committee categorize the institutional risk universe into institutional "A" risks and "B" risks. Oversight control of these "A" risks is the responsibility of the institutional compliance officer and that is the subject of Chapter 8. The risk area "A" risks that were not identified as significant for the institution are returned to the risk area responsible party for application of oversight controls. Each risk area responsible party then has the same responsibility for providing assurance of mitigation of noncompliance for these risk area "A" risks as the compliance officer has for the institution's "A" risks. Does this sound familiar? It should, because it is a repeat of what was said about work unit risks.

Since the only difference in the handling of "A" risks at the various organizational levels is the application of oversight controls, we need to clearly define that term. Oversight controls are those procedures applied to verify that for every "A" risk that is the responsibility of the specific management level there is (1) a designated responsible party, (2) a monitoring plan that is effectively operated, (3) a specialized training plan that is executed, (4) a reporting plan that is utilized, and (5) a predetermined set of consequences for instances of noncompliance that is followed. Table 13 above provides a guide to the application of oversight controls to the "A" risks at each level of the organization.

Lesson Learned

Because every identified "A" risk at any level of the organization is assigned through the above described technique to some management level for the application of oversight controls, all "A" risks, not just institution "A" risks, should be actively managed for the mitigation of noncompliance. By implication then, this means that the only compliance risks not actively managed through oversight controls are those that were not deemed significant at each level of the organization in which risk assessment was performed. Consequently, the use of the bottom-up risk assessment methodology provides the institution with the highest level of assurance that compliance risks are being managed to minimize instances of noncompliance.

CHAPTER 12
A LEARNING ORGANIZATION: MEASURE AND RENEW

Comparing the current status of the compliance program to the "action plan" for implementing the compliance program is the final step in the implementation of an effective compliance program. It is also the first step in the renewal of the compliance program. This is the link between what has happened and what will happen in the future. We will refer to this step as the learning step. Here we will measure how well the institution has done in actually implementing the original action plan to enhance institutional compliance. As we identify the gaps between what we planned and what we did, we will develop a revised plan to build upon the successes and eliminate the short-falls. This learning activity is accomplished through the self-assessment and external peer review process. The process has the following sub-processes: (1) develop the assessment instrument, (2) conduct a self-assessment of the compliance program, (3) undergo a peer review by an external team knowledgeable in higher education compliance, and (4) develop an action plan to address the peer review comments and improve the compliance program.

Develop the Assessment Instrument

The assessment instrument specifies the criteria by which the institutional compliance program will be measured and the procedures that will be used to gather the evidence needed to make those measurements. The most logical source of criteria to be used to measure the compliance program is the institution's action plan to enhance institutional compliance. Other sources of criteria are the essential elements of an institutional compliance program identified in the *Federal Sentencing Guidelines for Organizations* and the U.S. Department of Health and Human Services Office of Inspector General's *Guidelines for Hospitals*.

The University of Texas System Institutional Compliance Program self-assessment instrument is shown as Appendix J. This document used as its basic criteria the U.T. System *Action Plan*. Most of the procedures specified in the instrument are designed to provide information on the status of each prescribed step in the *Action Plan*. In fact, a reading of this document and the *Action Plan*, which is shown as Appendix B, will clearly illustrate the correlation between the two. In addition there are procedures in Appendix J to verify that the compliance program contains all of the elements prescribed by the *Federal Sentencing Guidelines for Organizations*.

The self-assessment instrument development is enhanced if it is performed jointly by the compliance function and the internal auditing function. The compliance function brings operational knowledge to the process and the internal auditing function brings knowledge of verification procedures, validation steps, and measurement options, and in addition, the internal auditing staff is knowledgeable about information gathering techniques. Additionally, the internal auditing function provides objectivity in the determination of content for the self-assessment.

Conduct a Self-assessment of the Compliance Program

Ideally. as part of the action plan, the chief executive officer will require the compliance program to undergo a self-assessment at least annually. The self-assessment process includes gathering pertinent information, drawing conclusions regarding the current status of the program, and reporting the results to the chief executive officer. There are four ways to perform this self-assessment. First, the compliance function, under the direction of the compliance officer, performs all the steps in the compliance self-assessment process. Second, the compliance officer, with the advice of the compliance committee, can appoint a subcommittee of the compliance committee to perform all the steps in the self-assessment process. Third, the chief executive officer and/or the compliance officer may contract with the internal auditing function to conduct the self-assessment. (This is usually a consulting service, not an assurance service.) Fourth, the compliance officer may appoint a team of knowledgeable individuals from within the institutional community, but not within the compliance infrastructure, to perform all the steps in the self-assessment process. Within the U.T. System, all four methods have been used by various components to conduct their respective self-assessments.

The instrument was piloted at one of the academic components of the U.T. System in December 1999 using a combination of compliance function personnel and internal auditing function staff. The component's executive management, compliance function, and "A" risks responsible parties recognized the value of the information produced by this process. As a result of the self-assessment, various parts of the compliance program at the component were revised, resulting in significant improvement in the program's overall effectiveness.

The U.T. System-wide compliance program and the System Administration compliance program had self-assessments conducted simultaneously by U.T. System Internal Audit Office staff. In addition, one of the U.T. health-related components chose to have the compliance officer and compliance function conduct their self-assessment. All three of these self-assessments resulted in a determination to request an external peer review of the respective compliance programs. Because of the decision to have an external peer review, no action plan was produced following the self-assessments. Individual improvements were implemented in anticipation of the peer review.

Lesson Learned

The self-assessment of the compliance program not only provides a scorecard for the program, but it also provides an indication of whether the compliance program implementation plan needs revising or whether an external peer review is required. A negative self-assessment requires a revised implementation plan. A positive self-assessment requires a second opinion — an external peer review. This second opinion is needed to combat the "rose-colored glasses" syndrome and provide independent, objective assurance to the chief executive officer on the status of the compliance program.

A self-assessment that reports substantial completion of all steps in the action plan and the existence of monitoring plans for a majority of the institution's "A" risks is a positive self-assessment. This positive self-assessment report requires the assurance provided by a second opinion — an external peer review. The benefits gained from the external peer review are (1) validation of the positive self-assessment report, (2) identification of any deficiencies not noted or reported in the self-assessment report, and (3) identification of resource allocation issues that are difficult for internal assessors to address. This second opinion is needed before an action plan is devised so that all areas requiring improvement are addressed. Once the external peer review report is received, the compliance officer will produce an action plan to address the noted areas needing improvement.

A self-assessment that reports completion of few steps in the action plan and/or the existence of few or no monitoring plans for institution "A" risks is deemed a negative self-assessment and indicates the need for revisions in the compliance program implementation plan. Under this condition, the compliance program would not benefit from a second opinion (external peer review). The institution does not need confirmation that it has failed to achieve a significant portion of compliance program goals and objectives. What it needs is a revised process for meeting goals and objectives. Therefore, the compliance management team (compliance officer, compliance committee, and compliance coordinator) should produce an action plan to address the deficiencies noted in the self-assessment.

One caution is in order. A positive self-assessment can include identification of areas needing improvement. Efforts to address the needed improvements should be made during the period between the self-assessment and the external peer review. In fact, the external peer review team will expect to find activity to address any deficiencies noted in the self-assessment. However, the compliance officer is not obligated to produce a formal action plan until after the peer review is completed.

Undergo an External Peer Review

A compliance program that receives a positive self-assessment should undergo an external peer review to validate the positive points in the self-assessment and to obtain objective support for any improvements identified in the self-assessment. The external peer review will provide assurance to the chief executive officer and the compliance officer that what is reported in the self-assessment is in fact the condition of the compliance program.

Preparation for the Peer Review

Preparation for the external peer review includes (1) selecting a team leader and at least three other team members, (2) developing a contract with the peer review team, (3) providing all team members with background information including the self-assessment, and (4) appointing an institutional liaison for the peer review team.

The team leader should be a person who has extensive knowledge in a broad range of compliance issues and who is the compliance officer at an institution with similar compliance risks. Other team members should have extensive knowledge in specific risk areas that are significant to the institution being reviewed. In the current environment, there are numerous individuals who meet these qualifications for the health-related activities of an institution of higher education. There are very few who would meet these qualifications on the academic side of higher education. Consequently, the search for peer review team leaders and members must go outside the compliance arena. The most logical place to find qualified individuals outside the compliance function is in the internal auditing function. Because of internal auditing's historical emphasis on compliance, this is a very fertile area in which to seek peer reviewers. The compensation for peer review team leaders and members is usually reimbursement of expenses.

Once a peer review team is designated, the compliance officer (with the advice of the compliance committee and the concurrence of the chief executive officer) should develop the peer review contract. This contract specifies the duties and responsibilities of the peer review team and the institution. It describes the criteria to which the program will be compared. It details the outcomes that the institution seeks and how these outcomes will be reported. The contract also specifies who will receive the final report. In addition, the contract should contain requirements concerning the confidentiality of information gathered during the review, and it should address the development and ownership of any working papers produced during the review. The peer review team leader and each member of the peer review team should sign the contract. The contract should also be signed by the institution's compliance officer and/or the chief executive officer. If a potential team member will not sign the contract, the compliance officer should choose a replacement.

While the negotiations are proceeding with the peer review team, the compliance officer should appoint a liaison to the team who will accumulate all pertinent information and provide it to the team members in advance. This information should include at least the action plan for the compliance program, the completed self-assessment, minutes of compliance committee meetings, copies of monitoring plans, the general compliance training plan, the institutional risk assessment, and reports from all assurance activities that have been completed. If the volume of information seems excessive, the compliance officer and the peer review team leader should agree on what will be provided to all team members in advance of their site visit. The liaison will also support the peer review team while they are on site at the institution. This usually includes arranging interviews, providing transportation and clerical support, and any other services that will facilitate the activities of the team.

Conduct of the Peer Review

The peer review team leader should develop a peer review program to address the contract requirements. This program will usually concentrate on the review of documentation that supports the self-assessment and on interviews with selected personnel in the compliance program. Peer review interview teams are always composed of two peer review team members. Document analysis may be done individually or jointly by peer review team members. Each team leader will have their own style for reaching conclusions and for preparing information for the report.

The peer review team will be on site at the institution from one to three days. At the end of the onsite portion of the review, the team leader should make an oral report to the chief executive officer and the compliance officer, even if a formal written report is to follow. If a formal written report is required by the peer review contract, that report should be submitted to the designated recipient within two weeks of the end of the onsite phase. All notes, working papers, and other documents generated by the peer review team should be disposed of at the end of the onsite phase in accordance with the peer review contract.

Develop an Action Plan

The learning step concludes with an action plan to address the areas of improvement noted in either the self-assessment report (negative self-assessment) or the peer review report (positive self-assessment). This action plan specifies what the compliance program management will do to improve the institution's ability to minimize instances of noncompliance, or perhaps a better way to put it, to maximize success. The action plan should address each situation noted in the self-assessment report or the peer review report. It will include what is to be done, who is responsible for doing it, and when it will be completed. Technically, this is a revision of the originally adopted action plan to enhance institutional compliance. As such, it must be incorporated into any future self-assessment instrument. The action plan should be filed with the same institution official who received the self-assessment report or the peer review report, normally the chief executive officer.

Lesson Learned

Experience has taught that the most important step in the peer review process is the contract with the peer review team. There must be a very clear definition of the duties and responsibilities of the team, the type of final report that will be issued and to whom it will be issued, and the confidentiality of information. The peer review team members are protected and the institution is protected.

Summary

It is easy to be caught up in the day-to-day activities of implementing an effective compliance program. In fact, we can become so "doing" oriented that we fail to stop and take stock of what we have actually accomplished. The annual self-assessment requirement is our trigger to stop and take stock. Whatever method is used to perform the self-assessment, it is imperative that the individuals involved back away from the details of compliance and take a holistic look at the program. Individual steps may seem to be working very well when looked at as separate activities. However, when viewed as part of a larger universe, they may not be making the optimal contribution to success. It is only through this self-examination and validation process that the compliance officer can really know whether or not the program is moving toward achievement of its objectives.

This is the final chapter, the final step in the implementation of an effective compliance program. You have gone from need recognition to development of a plan of action, to creation of an infrastructure, to managing risks, to validating results, to dealing with noncompliance, to assessing accomplishments. You have completed the cycle. You are done! You are just beginning! It is time to go back to Chapter 1 and do it again!

The Institute of Internal Auditors Research Foundation

APPENDIX A
EFFECTIVE COMPLIANCE SYSTEMS CONFERENCE PROGRAM

March 20 - 21, 2001
The Thompson Conference Center
The University of Texas at Austin
Austin, Texas

Day 1 - March 20, 2001

3:00 - 4: 15 p.m.   Who Needs a Compliance Program and Why?
Panel Discussion
Moderator: Dr. Urton Anderson, Clark W. Thompson, Jr., Professor of
Accounting Education and Associate Dean for Undergraduate Programs,
The University of Texas at Austin
Panel:
Mr. Odell Guyton, JD, Corporate Compliance Officer,
University of Pennsylvania
Mr. Steven M. Jung, Director of Internal Audit, Stanford University
Mr. Charles G. Chaffin, System-wide Compliance Officer,
The University of Texas System

4:15 - 5:00 p.m.   How to Start – An Action Plan to Ensure Compliance
Moderator: Mr. John Roan, Executive Vice President for Business Affairs,
The University of Texas Southwestern Medical Center at Dallas
Presenter: Mr. Scott L. Scarborough, Vice President for Business Affairs
and Compliance Officer, The University of Texas at Tyler

5:30 - 6:30 p.m.   High-risk Area Roundtables and Cocktails
Medical Billing
Mr. Dieter Lehnortt, Director, Medical Billing Compliance Office,
The University of Texas Southwestern Medical Center at Dallas
Clinical Research
Dr. Carleen Brunelli, Chief Research and Regulatory Affairs Officer,
The University of Texas M. D. Anderson Cancer Center Basic

The Institute of Internal Auditors Research Foundation

Research
    Dr. Juan Sanchez, Vice President for Research, The University of Texas at Austin
Environmental Health & Safety
    Mr. Kim Smith, Director of Safety, Health and Environmental Services, The University of Texas Health Center at Tyler
NCAA
    Ms. Lynn Hickey, Athletic Director, The University of Texas at San Antonio
Student Financial Aid
    Dr. Richard Padilla, Vice President for Student Affairs, The University of Texas at El Paso
HIPAA
    Dr. James Guckian, Vice Chancellor for Health Affairs, The University of Texas System
Conflict of Interest
    Ms. Carrie King, JD, Chief Compliance Officer, The University of Texas M. D. Anderson Cancer Center
Human Resources
    Mr. Anthony Ramirez, Director of Human Resources, The University of Texas Health Science Center at San Antonio

6:30 - 8:30 p.m.   Dinner
    Keynote Speaker:
    Dr. Robert Witt, President, The University of Texas at Arlington

Day 2 - March 21, 2001

8:00 - 8:45 a.m.   Elements of a Successful Compliance Program
    Moderator: Mr. Charles G. Chaffin, System-wide Compliance Officer
    The University of Texas System
    Presenter: Mr. Odell Guyton, JD, Corporate Compliance Officer, The University of Pennsylvania

8:45 - 9:45 a.m.   Code of Conduct and General Compliance Training
    Moderator: Mr. David B. Crawford, Manager of Audits, The University of Texas System
    Presenters:
    Mr. Kerry Kennedy, Executive Vice-Chancellor for Business Affairs, The University of Texas System

Ms. Nancy Gast, Executive Director Institutional Compliance,
The University of Texas Medical Branch at Galveston
Ms. Carrie King, JD, Chief Compliance Officer,
The University of Texas M.D. Anderson Cancer Center

9:45 - 10:00 a.m. Break

10:00 - 11:00 a.m. Risk-assessment and Monitoring Plans
Moderator: Mr. Paul M. Henry, Special Assistant for Management and
Compliance - Health Affairs - The University of Texas System
Presenters:
Dr. John W. Sparks, Physician in Chief and Medical Billing Compliance
Officer, The University of Texas Health Science Center – Houston
Ms. Angela Wishon, JD, Director for Research Facilitation and
Compliance, The University of Texas Medical Branch at Galveston

11:00 - 11:50 a.m. Breakout Sessions (Hands-on Demonstrations)
Code of Conduct and Confidential Reporting Mechanism
General Compliance Training Delivery Mechanisms
Examples of Ways to Communicate Compliance

12:00 - 1:00 p.m. Lunch

1:00 - 1:45 p.m.   Allocation of Resources/Chief Executive Officer Commitment
Moderator: Mr. Kerry L. Kennedy, Executive Vice Chancellor for Business
Affairs, The University of Texas System
Presenters:
Mr. R.D. Burck, Chancellor, The University of Texas System
Dr. Ricardo Romo, President, The University of Texas at San Antonio
Mr. Leon Leach, Executive Vice President,
The University of Texas M. D. Anderson Cancer Center

Day 2 -March 21, 2001

1:45 - 2:45 p.m.   Assurance Activities
      Moderator: Dr. Urton Anderson, Clark W. Thompson, Jr.,
        Professor of Accounting, Education and Associate Dean for
        Undergraduate Programs, The University of Texas at Austin
      Presenters:
      Audits and Agreed-upon Procedures
        Mr. J. Michael Peppers, Director, Audit Services,
          The University of Texas Medical Branch at Galveston
      Certification and Inspection
        Mr. David Larson, Vice President for Business Affairs,
          The University of Texas at San Antonio
      Peer Reviews
        Ms. Sharron Devere, Assistant Vice President and Chief Compliance
          Officer, The University of Texas Health Science Center at Houston
      External Reviews and Audits
        Ms. Gayle Knight, Assistant Vice President for Institutional Compliance,
          The University of Texas Health Science Center at San Antonio

2:45 - 3:00 p.m.   Closing Remarks

The Institute of Internal Auditors Research Foundation

APPENDIX B
ACTION PLAN TO ENSURE
INSTITUTIONAL COMPLIANCE

THE UNIVERSITY OF TEXAS SYSTEM
1998

APPROVED BY THE CHANCELLOR AND PRESENTED TO THE BUSINESS AFFAIRS
AND AUDIT COMMITTEE OF THE BOARD OF REGENTS ON APRIL 24, 1998.

The Institute of Internal Auditors Research Foundation

INTRODUCTION

On January 16, 1998, the Chairman of The University of Texas System (U. T. System) Board of Regents requested that the Chancellor create an Ad Hoc Committee to develop an Action Plan to ensure U. T. System compliance with applicable laws, regulations, policies, and procedures. The Chairman requested that the Action Plan include an appropriate governance structure and that it designate the appropriate officer who would be responsible to the Board of Regents for system-wide compliance.

On January 23, 1998, the Chancellor asked Mr. R. D. Burck, Executive Vice Chancellor for Business Affairs, to chair a system-wide Ad Hoc Committee on Institutional Compliance. The Ad Hoc Committee met at The University of Texas Health Science Center at Houston on March 2, 1998. The meeting featured a three-hour presentation by representatives of Deloitte & Touche LLP entitled, "Corporate Compliance for Universities and Academic Medical Centers." After the presentation, the Ad Hoc Committee discussed the requisite elements of a U. T. System Action Plan to Ensure Institutional Compliance (Compliance Action Plan). Since the meeting on March 2, the Compliance Action Plan has been circulated to all members of the Ad Hoc Committee for review and comment.

The following pages present the 1998 Action Plan items by "Responsible Party." The Action Plan includes the following key elements:

- Designation of the Executive Vice Chancellor for Business Affairs as the U.T. System-wide Compliance Officer.
- The appointment of an Institutional Compliance Officer at System Administration and at each component institution by June 1, 1998.
- The creation of a U.T. System-wide Compliance Committee and parallel Compliance Committees at System Administration and each component institution which meet at least quarterly.
- The mandate for a *continuous and proactive* compliance function which reports to the Institutional Compliance Officer at System Administration and each component institution.
- The allocation of sufficient resources at System Administration and at each component institution to fund compliance activities (including information resources, training, and monitoring activities) that reduce compliance risk to a reasonably low level.

- The requirement that the Institutional Compliance Officers and Committees at System Administration and the component institutions report their activities to the U. T. System-wide Compliance Officer at least quarterly.

The Ad Hoc Committee believes that it is important to clearly distinguish responsibility and accountability for compliance with laws, regulations, policies, and procedures as follows:

- The U.T. System-wide Compliance Officer is responsible and will be held accountable for apprising the Chancellor and the Board of Regents of the institutional compliance functions and activities at System Administration and at each of the component institutions.
- The Institutional Compliance Officers at System Administration and at each component institution are responsible and will be held accountable for a risk-based process that builds compliance consciousness into daily business processes, monitors the effectiveness of those processes and communicates instances of non-compliance to appropriate administrative officers for corrective, restorative and/or disciplinary action.
- Responsibility for actual compliance with laws, regulations, policies, and procedures rests with each individual employee. Accountability resides primarily with the department head of each operating unit.
- The Chancellor and each Chief Administrative Officer are responsible and will be held accountable for the sufficiency of resources allocated to compliance activities and the appropriateness of corrective and disciplinary action taken in the event of non-compliance.
- Internal Audit is responsible and will be held accountable for independently evaluating the design and effectiveness of the compliance function at System Administration and each component institution on both an annual and an ongoing basis and for making recommendations for improvements to the Institutional Compliance Officers at System Administration and at each component institution.

The Ad Hoc Committee believes that the implementation of this Compliance Action Plan will significantly improve U. T. System compliance. As such, we respectfully submit this Compliance Action Plan to the Chancellor for his review and approval.

Ad Hoc Committee on Institutional Compliance
March 1998

The Institute of Internal Auditors Research Foundation

Action Plan - Institutional Compliance

Action Item	Responsible Party	Due Date
1. Adopt a Board of Regents' resolution on institutional compliance. *Implementation Guidance: Board resolution on institutional compliance.*	Board of Regents	May 14, 1998
2. Designate the Executive Vice Chancellor for Business Affairs as the U. T. System-wide Compliance Officer *Implementation Guidance: The Executive Vice Chancellor for Business Affairs shall be responsible to the Chancellor and the Board for the System-wide compliance function.*	Chancellor	May 14, 1998
3. Designate a Compliance Officer at System Administration and at each component institution. *Implementation Guidance: In most cases, the Institutional Compliance Officer should be the Chief Business Officer or a high-ranking administrative official at the component institution.*	Chancellor Chief Administrative Officer	June 1, 1998
4. Appoint a System-wide Compliance Committee and a Committee at System Administration and each component institution. *Implementation Guidance: At least two approaches may be used to form the Institutional Compliance Committee. 1) appoint a cross-functional team from operating units with high-risk compliance issues (areas to be considered include accreditation; employment; student related; sponsored research; endowment; athletics; environmental health and safety; tax related; health care billing and confidentiality; law enforcement; facilities; and other compliance requirements). Under this approach, the Institutional Compliance Officer should chair the Committee.*	Chancellor Chief Administrative Officer	June 1, 1998

The Institute of Internal Auditors Research Foundation

Action Item	Responsible Party	Due Date
2) expand the role of the Institutional Audit Committee to include Institutional Compliance and change/ enhance membership as necessary. Generally, this approach assumes a separate institutional compliance function that reports to the Institutional Compliance Officer.		
5. Require the Institutional Compliance Committee to meet at least quarterly.	Chancellor Chief Administrative Officer	August 31, 1998
6. Organize, fund, and provide oversight to an ongoing and proactive compliance function which meets the criteria of the U.S. Sentencing Guidelines that reports to the Institutional Compliance Officer at System Administration and each component institution. *Implementation Guidance: At least two approaches may be used to organize a compliance function at each institution: (1) If the institution uses a cross-functional team as its Institutional Compliance Committee, then the responsibility of planning, organizing, directing, and controlling compliance activities rests with the Committee itself. (2) a separately staffed compliance function is responsible for the planning, organizing, directing, and controlling of compliance activities. Under this approach, the activities of the dedicated compliance function are regularly reported to the Institutional Compliance Committee.*	Chancellor Chief Administrative Officer	September 1, 1998
7. Budget sufficient resources to fund ongoing and continuous compliance activities (information resources, training, and monitoring activities) that reduce compliance risk to an acceptably low level. *Implementation Guidance: The amount of funding necessary for compliance activities depends on the size of the component institution and its associated compliance risks. The allocation of the funding depends on the organizational structure of the*	Chancellor Chief Administrative Officer	September 1, 1998

Action Item	Responsible Party	Due Date
compliance function (see action items 4 and 6). It is understood that risk cannot be reduced to zero. However, it should be reduced to a reasonably low level. Funding must be provided for: 1) assuring good information resources to keep current on regulatory changes and interpretations; 2) extensive in-house or external-based training programs which provide both general compliance training to all employees on an annual basis, and ongoing specialized training tailored to the needs of each employee who has job responsibilities in areas of significant risk; and 3) ongoing monitoring activities which provide management vital information on the degree to which the component institution complies with laws, regulations, policies, and procedures.(Monitoring should generally be provided at three levels: within daily business processes; through the institutional compliance function; and through internal audits).		
8. Submit an annual risk-based plan of compliance activities to the U. T. System-wide Compliance Officer for review and approval. *Implementation Guidance: The first step in developing this plan is accumulating a compliance universe document which presents details of laws, regulations, policies, and procedures to which System Administration and the component institutions are subject (this includes federal, state, local, UT and institutional obligations). Next, the compliance group must assess the risk of noncompliance for all elements in the universe. Generally, the risk model should consider both the financial and embarrassment risks of noncompliance and should also candidly self-assess existing skill levels, compliance consciousness and recent histories of alleged or known noncompliant behavior. The annual risk-based plan should summarize this process by providing a listing of all significant compliance requirements and a summary assessment (e.g. high, moderate, low) of the risk of*	Institutional Compliance Officer	October 31, 1998

The Institute of Internal Auditors Research Foundation

Action Item	Responsible Party	Due Date
noncompliance. Based on the risk assessment, the plan should describe the institution's compliance activities that will reduce the risks to reasonably low levels. *The effectiveness of the institutional compliance plan may be judged by documented evidence of restorative action (i.e. self-reporting of errors and repayment of monies received in error); and evidence of disciplinary action taken against employees found to have engaged in noncompliant behavior as well as those who improperly failed to detect such behavior.* *The annual risk-based plan must present detail of how a combination of employee training and awareness programs, monitoring mechanisms, and changes in policies and procedures will equip all employees to understand their compliance obligations, set clear expectations for appropriate employee behavior, and provide insight into the ramifications of noncompliance. In the final analysis, the plan should demonstrate how each employee will become empowered to take an active role in reducing institutional risk.*		
9. Establish functional liaisons and develop a support structure sufficient to ensure accomplishment of the plan for each activity that is deemed to be high risk (e.g. the already established medical billing and record keeping functions at medical components; environmental health and safety; and NCAA, etc.). *Implementation Guidance:* While to a certain extent this *may be a matter of coordinating existing resources and enhancing compliance-related activities, each risk area must have a formally established and documented compliance function to: obtain and disseminate information; develop and administer training; and monitor effectiveness. In many cases this may require the establishment of subcommittees each of which will focus on one particular high-risk area.*	Chief Administrative Officer with input from the Institutional Compliance Officer and Institutional Compliance Committee	October 31, 1998

Action Item	Responsible Party	Due Date
10. Ensure that appropriate general compliance training for all employees and specialized compliance training for employees whose job responsibilities involve them in high-compliance-risk activities are being provided on a regular basis and that attendance levels are acceptable. *Implementation Guidance: Availability and attendance records are key monitoring data that should be provided to and considered by the Compliance Committee at every quarterly meeting.*	Institutional Compliance Officer	January 1, 1999
11. Submit a quarterly report on compliance activities to the U.T. System-wide Compliance Officer. *Implementation Guidance: The quarterly report should compare progress to date with the annual risk-based plan, and should indicate areas where additional emphasis is required. Instances where initial investigation indicates probable cause to suspect significant noncompliance should be communicated to the U.T. System-wide Compliance Officer and the Office of General Counsel, if appropriate. The report format will be determined by the U.T. System-wide Compliance Officer.*	Institutional Compliance Officer	First quarterly report (for the qtr ending 11/30/98) is due by December 15, 1998
12. Follow-up to determine that appropriate corrective, restorative and/or disciplinary action has been taken in the event of noncompliance. *Implementation Guidance: The principal responsibilities of the Institutional Compliance Committee are: to ensure that compliance activities are appropriately risk-based; to continuously assess and assure the effectiveness of the program; to keep the Chancellor and the Chief Administrative Officer aware of compliance risks, activities, and findings; and to ensure that the dissemination of information regarding compliance matters is not restricted. The discharge of these responsibilities includes discussion of potential areas of noncompliance and ensuring that appropriate*	Institutional Compliance Committee Chief Administrative Officer	November 30, 1998

The Institute of Internal Auditors Research Foundation

Action Item	Responsible Party	Due Date
corrective, restorative, and disciplinary actions are taken in the event of noncompliance. If the Institutional Compliance Officer believes that the appropriate administratively-accountable party has not followed relevant policies and procedures regarding corrective, restorative, and/or disciplinary action, then the Institutional Compliance Officer should report his or her concerns to the Chief Administrative Officer. At that point, the Chief Administrative Officer is responsible for the appropriateness of the actions taken to resolve the compliance issue.		
13. Establish a confidential mechanism that allows employees to obtain information regarding compliance issues and/or report instances of suspected noncompliance outside of the normal chain of command and in a manner that preserves confidentiality and assures nonretaliation. *Implementation Guidance: The most common and acceptable methods of providing such a mechanism are the establishment of a compliance telephone hotline or post office box at System Administration and each component institution. The key elements of these confidential mechanism programs include written documentation of all notifications received; a prompt cross-functional consultation and triage function (generally involving high ranking representatives from the legal, security, internal audit, and human resources areas) to determine the need for and nature of appropriate investigative action; follow-up to assure timely and appropriate resolution of issues; and documentation of the ultimate disposition of all calls received. It is critical that the Office of General Counsel and institutional counsel be initially and continuously involved in both establishing and maintaining this function.*	Institutional Compliance Officer	September 1, 1998

The Institute of Internal Auditors Research Foundation

Action Item	Responsible Party	Due Date
14. Develop a compliance manual which provides documentation of management's considerations of compliance, sets forth expectations and standards of conduct, and outlines methodologies to be employed to annually assess the effectiveness of the plan and each Institutional Compliance Officer. *Implementation Guidance: A manual should generally document the compliance structure; include copies of relevant documents, charters and policies; show examples of monitoring and reporting activities and forms; and document the process for evaluating Compliance Officers and for the Compliance Committee to annually self-assess its performance.*	Institutional Compliance Officer Institutional Compliance Committee	September 1, 1998
15. Annually audit the design and the effectiveness of the U.T. System compliance function and the compliance function at System Administration and the component institutions. *Implementation Guidance: In its audit plan, Internal Audit should include audit(s) of the design and effectiveness of the compliance function both System-wide (System Audit Office) and at System Administration (System Audit Office) and each component institution (institutional Internal Audit Office). Based on the audit(s), recommendations for improvements should be made to the Institutional Compliance Officer. The Compliance Officer will be responsible for responding to such recommendations by developing action plans and timetables for remedial action to be approved by the Compliance Committee, which will be responsible for follow-up to ensure timely resolution.*	Director of Internal Audit	Initial design audit to be completed by November 30, 1998
16. Summary information on hotline or post office box activities should be presented at every Compliance Committee meeting.	Institutional Compliance Officer	First report in 2nd Quarter of fiscal 1999

APPENDIX C

COMPARISON OF FEDERAL SENTENCING GUIDELINES, OIG GUIDELINES, AND U.T. SYSTEM ACTION PLAN TO ENSURE INSTITUTIONAL COMPLIANCE

CRITERIA	U.T. SYSTEM ACTION PLAN	FEDERAL SENTENCING GUIDELINES	OIG GUIDELINES FOR HOSPITALS, ETC.
Written policies and procedures	**Step 14** Develop a compliance manual which provides documentation of management's considerations of compliance, sets forth expectations and standards of conduct and outlines methodologies to be employed to annually assess the effectiveness of the plan and the compliance officer	Compliance standards and procedures	Written policies and procedures, including a standard of conduct
Designated high-level manager as responsible for compliance program	**Step 2** System-wide compliance officer **Step 3** Component and System Administration compliance officers	Specific individual within high-level personnel of the organization must have been assigned overall responsibility to oversee compliance with the standards and procedures	Designation of a compliance officer responsible for operating and monitoring the compliance program
Training	**Step 10** Ensure that appropriate general compliance training for all employees and specialized training for appropriate employees is provided on a regular basis	Communicate effectively its standards and procedures to all employees and other agents by requiring participation in training and by disseminating publications explaining the program	Regular employee education and training programs
Auditing and Monitoring	**Step 9** Establish ....and develop a support structure to ensure accomplishment of the plan for each activity that is deemed high-risk		

The Institute of Internal Auditors Research Foundation

CRITERIA	U.T. SYSTEM ACTION PLAN	FEDERAL SENTENCING GUIDELINES	OIG GUIDELINES FOR HOSPITALS, ETC.
	Step 15 Annually audit the design and effectiveness of the U.T. System compliance function and the compliance function at System Administration and the component institutions	Auditing and monitoring	Periodic audits to monitor compliance
Anonymous reporting mechanism	**Step 13** Establish a confidential reporting mechanism	A method of reporting noncompliance without fear of retribution	A reporting mechanism to receive complaints anonymously
Consistent discipline for noncompliance	**Step 12** Follow-up to determine that appropriate corrective, restorative, and/or disciplinary action has been taken in the event of noncompliance	Standards must be consistently enforced through appropriate discipline of responsible individuals	Corrective action policies and procedures, including disciplinary policies, to respond to allegations of noncompliance
Reasonable steps to correct any identified problems with compliance	**Step 12** (see above)	After noncompliance is reported the organization must take reasonable steps to respond and prevent	Investigation and correction of identified systemic problems, including policies addressing the non-employment of sanctioned individuals

The Institute of Internal Auditors Research Foundation

APPENDIX D

Implementing an Institutional Compliance Program at Stanford:
A "Matrix" Approach

Background

A comprehensive institutional compliance program is one which integrates and coordinates all significant requirements with which the institution must comply by law, regulation, or other binding rule or agreement. Comprehensive organizational compliance programs are common in highly regulated industries, and have become less rare recently in higher education as a result of highly publicized instances of alleged noncompliance in such areas as Medicare billing (e.g., Corporate Integrity Agreement imposed on the University of Pennsylvania by the Department of Justice).

In 1987, the Federal Sentencing Guidelines (FSG) provided one of the first "models" for organizational compliance programs. They recommended that federal judges give "credit" for reduced penalties to organizations found guilty of violations <u>if</u> they had previously developed "an effective program to prevent and detect violations of law." Attachment A provides the definition of such a program from the FSG Section 8A1.2.

In 1998, in response to the PATH investigations at university teaching hospitals, models based on the FSG were developed by the Department of Health and Human Services (DHHS) Office of Inspector General (OIG) (http://www.dhhs.gov/progorg/oig/modcomp/hospital.pdf). A December 2000 survey of 17 university Chief Financial Officers indicated that formal compliance programs had been or were being established at 10 of the universities; many of these programs were initiated as a result of adoption of one or more elements of the DHHS/OIG model within their Medical Centers. An article in recent issues of the journal of the National Association of College and University Business Officers (NACUBO) provides an overview of such programs (see Spring 2000 issues of the NACUBO journal at http://www.nacubo.org/website/members/bomag/00/01/ compliance.html).

All these models contain various components aimed at enhancing and ensuring institutional compliance, including:

- Establishing institutional expectations and codes of conduct
- Developing and effectively communicating policies and procedures
- Designating a formal compliance office with suitable administrative powers
- Implementing a program to monitor compliance
- Identifying and applying sanctions for intentional noncompliance

A Suggested "Matrix" Framework for Stanford's Institutional Compliance Program

Currently at Stanford, programs containing components such as those bulleted above have evolved in a number of specific compliance areas (e.g., Environmental Health and Safety, sexual harassment, NCAA rules, research administration), but there is no single point of contact. This document provides a plan to initiate development of a "matrix" compliance program which connects these individual components, coordinates their operations, and represents the University's institutional perspective, but at the same time avoids the creation of a new bureaucracy which could be perceived by the faculty as unhelpful. We call this a "matrix" framework, because its goal is to enhance compliance primarily through the actions of a decentralized matrix of University offices and officers, coordinated and assisted by a small central compliance function with a reporting relationship to the Stanford University Board of Trustees.

Attachments B and C provide an overview of the "matrix," showing the compliance components we believe should be included (rows of Attachment B), compliance areas (i.e., clusters of laws, regulations, contractual requirements) to be included (the 16 columns of Attachment B), and suggested offices and individuals to be incorporated within the matrix (columns of Attachment C).

Proposed Implementation Steps

1. President redesignates the Director of Internal Audit as the Director of Internal Audit and Institutional Compliance (the Director). Director continues to report to the CFO, with a direct reporting relationship to the President and the Committee on Audit of the Board of Trustees.

2. Board of Trustees redesignates the Committee on Audit as the Committee on Audit and Compliance.

3. Director of Internal Audit and Compliance is tasked with presentation of an annual institutional compliance report to the President, Cabinet, and Committee on Audit and Compliance.

4. President and Provost appoint a Compliance Oversight Committee, staffed by the Director, made up of the persons functionally responsible for compliance in the 16 "matrix" areas (fourth column in Attachment C plus representatives of the General Counsel's Office and the administrative deans from the schools). The primary purpose of this Committee would be to meet at least semiannually to do risk assessments and ensure that all members are knowledgeable about pertinent noncompliance risks deriving from sources external to the University or from any one of the other 16 areas. Committee members would also be responsible for consulting with and keeping the policy makers in the 16 areas (second column in Attachment C) appraised of compliance issues within their areas.

5. Director initiates Compliance Program activities, including:

   - Works with the Compliance Coordinating Committee to ensure that each cell of the "compliance matrix" (Attachment B) contains appropriate policies and processes and that the existence of policies or processes in that area is documented.[1]
   - Promotes compliance awareness through "ethics initiatives," either University-wide, or in concert with the faculty and staff training programs of the offices in the compliance "matrix."
   - Provides liaison with the Office of the General Counsel, the Office of University Communications, and other responsible offices in addressing incidents of alleged noncompliance that arise.
   - Works through the Internal Audit function to both monitor compliance and assess the adequacy of compliance activities in each area of the matrix. Includes such information in the annual compliance report.
   - Implements and publicizes a "Compliance Help Line" program, which Stanford employees who have concerns of any kind stemming from possible noncompliance could call to register their concerns, anonymously if desired. (This help line could be internally staffed or could be contracted out to another organization — there are several which specialize in offering this service. Call content will be documented and reviewed; calls pertaining to any of the 16 areas in the "matrix" will be forwarded to the responsible offices for handling, with later follow-up by the Director.)

---

[1]This is critical to success of this model; in essence, the idea is to push most of the compliance activity "out" to the existing offices in the matrix, rather than doing it centrally.

The Institute of Internal Auditors Research Foundation

- Networks with other university compliance officers throughout the nation to keep apprised of emerging compliance issues, share best practices, etc.
- Considers needed additions to the compliance matrix, if other important areas of compliance are identified, and keeps the matrix up-to-date, as Stanford's organization changes and new individuals assume roles of responsibility.
- Considers needed changes in the compliance program and brings them to Compliance Oversight Committee for review and transmittal to the President.
- In cooperation with the Office of the General Counsel, develops a formal policy, and procedures, to protect University employees who make allegations of noncompliance.
- Secures necessary funding from the Provost to carry out the above activities.

Attachment A
Excerpt from Federal Sentencing Guidelines
§8A1.2. Application Instructions - Organizations

(k) An "effective program to prevent and detect violations of law" means a program that has been reasonably designed, implemented, and enforced so that it generally will be effective in preventing and detecting criminal conduct. Failure to prevent or detect the instant offense, by itself, does not mean that the program was not effective. The hallmark of an effective program to prevent and detect violations of law is that the organization exercised due diligence in seeking to prevent and detect criminal conduct by its employees and other agents. Due diligence requires at a minimum that the organization must have taken the following types of steps:

(1) The organization must have established compliance standards and procedures to be followed by its employees and other agents that are reasonably capable of reducing the prospect of criminal conduct.

(2) Specific individual(s) within high-level personnel of the organization must have been assigned overall responsibility to oversee compliance with such standards and procedures.

(3) The organization must have used due care not to delegate substantial discretionary authority to individuals whom the organization knew, or should have known through the exercise of due diligence, had a propensity to engage in illegal activities.

(4) The organization must have taken steps to communicate effectively its standards and procedures to all employees and other agents, e.g., by requiring participation in training programs or by disseminating publications that explain in a practical manner what is required.

(5) The organization must have taken reasonable steps to achieve compliance with its standards, e.g., by utilizing monitoring and auditing systems reasonably designed to detect criminal conduct by its employees and other agents and by having in place and publicizing a reporting system whereby employees and other agents could report criminal conduct by others within the organization without fear of retribution.

(6) The standards must have been consistently enforced through appropriate disciplinary mechanisms, including, as appropriate, discipline of individuals responsible for the failure to detect an offense. Adequate discipline of individuals responsible for an offense is a necessary component of enforcement; however, the form of discipline that will be appropriate will be case specific.

(7) After an offense has been detected, the organization must have taken all reasonable steps to respond appropriately to the offense and to prevent further similar offenses — including any necessary modifications to its program to prevent and detect violations of law.

The precise actions necessary for an effective program to prevent and detect violations of law will depend upon a number of factors. Among the relevant factors are:

(i) Size of the organization — The requisite degree of formality of a program to prevent and detect violations of law will vary with the size of the organization: the larger the organization, the more formal the program typically should be. A larger organization generally should have established written policies defining the standards and procedures to be followed by its employees and other agents.

(ii) Likelihood that certain offenses may occur because of the nature of its business — If because of the nature of an organization's business there is a substantial risk that certain types of offenses may occur, management must have taken steps to prevent and detect those types of offenses. For example, if an organization handles toxic substances, it must have established standards and procedures designed to ensure that those substances are properly handled at all times. If an organization employs sales personnel who have flexibility in setting prices, it must have established standards and procedures designed to prevent and detect price-fixing. If an organization employs sales personnel who have flexibility to represent the material characteristics of a product, it must have established standards and procedures designed to prevent fraud.

(iii) Prior history of the organization — An organization's prior history may indicate types of offenses that it should have taken actions to prevent. Recurrence of misconduct similar to that which an organization has previously committed casts doubt on whether it took all reasonable steps to prevent such misconduct.

An organization's failure to incorporate and follow applicable industry practice or the standards called for by any applicable governmental regulation weighs against a finding of an effective program to prevent and detect violations of law.

Historical Note: Effective November 1, 1991 (see Appendix C, amendment 422); November 1, 1997 (see Appendix C, amendment 546).

Attachment B
Compliance Matrix: Components of Stanford Institutional Compliance Program and Compliance Areas

Compliance Areas	EH&S (incl Health Physics)	Medicare Billing	Research	Research Admin	Scientific Misconduct	Human/Animal Subjects	HR/EEOC (incl sexual harassment)	ADA	NCAA	Fire and Bldg Safety	IRS and CA Tax	Donor Gift Restrictions	Faculty & Staff Conflict of Interest	Immigration	Technology Licensing	Land Use
Essential components of compliance program																
Written institutional code of ethics and conduct																
Explicitly stated compliance policies and standards																
Training for all employees on code of ethics and compliance policies and standards related to their jobs																
Designation of a responsible institutional officer w/ appropriate powers and expertise																
Adoption/provision of adequate procedures, resources, and systems to permit compliance																
Maintenance of a process to allow anonymous reporting of alleged noncompliance																
Protection for employees who lodge reports																
Regular monitoring and auditing to test compliance																
Mechanisms to enforce rules and discipline rule violators																
Management commitment to take corrective actions and follow up to ensure effectiveness of corrective actions																
System to communicate effective actions and follow up undertaken																
Adequate board-level oversight of compliance function																
Mechanisms to communicate the impact of rules to the creators and enforcers of the rules																

The Institute of Internal Auditors Research Foundation

Attachment C
Stanford University Offices/Officers Responsible for Compliance Areas

Offices/Officers	Cognizant Policy Office	Cognizant Officer	Functionally Responsible Office	Functionally Responsible Person(s)*	Primary Focus of Responsibility
Compliance Areas					
EH&S	Dean of Research & Grad Policy		Environmental Health & Safety Office		PI's
Medicare/Medical Billing	VP for Medical Affairs		SHC Compliance Office		Med Faculty / SHC Compliance Office
Research	Dean of Research & Grad Policy		Office of the Dean of Research		PI's / Committee on Research
Research Administration	Associate Vice President (AVP) for Research Administration		Office of Research Administration		PI's / Departmental and School Administrators / Office of Research Administration
Scientific Misconduct	Dean of Research & Grad Policy		Office of the Dean of Research / Offices of the School Deans		
Human/Animal Subjects	Dean of Research & Grad Policy		Administrative Panels, Compliance Office		PI's
HR/EEOC	VP for Business Affairs and CFO		Human Resources		Departments, Central HR
ADA	VP for Land & Buildings		Facilities Operations		Building Administrators
NCAA	Provost		DAPER		Coaches
Fire and Bldg Safety	VP for Land & Buildings		EH&S/Fire Marshal		EH&S/Schools/Departments
IRS and CA Tax	VP for Business Affairs and CFO		Controller		Controller's Office FAIR Group
Donor Gift Restrictions	President		Office of Development		Schools/Departments/Faculty
Conflicts of Interest	Provost		Dean of Research & Grad Policy, VP for Business Affairs and CFO		Schools/Faculty, Controller, Director of Procurement
Immigration	VP for Business Affairs and CFO		Human Resources		Departments, Central HR
Technology Licensing/ Intellectual Property	Dean of Research & Grad Policy		Office of Technology Licensing		OTL, Faculty
Land Use	VP for Land & Buildings		SMC/CP&M		SMC/CP&M

*Note: The school administrative deans also have functional responsibilities in most areas.

The Institute of Internal Auditors Research Foundation

APPENDIX E
COMPLIANCE RISK PROFILE FOR
HIGHER EDUCATION

Risk Area	Academic	Health-Related
Student Welfare	X	X
Patient Care		X
Billing for Services		X
Funding Formulas	X	X
Human Resources	X	X
Fiscal Management	X	X
Environmental Health & Safety	X	X
Accreditation	X	X
Infection Control		X
Research – Basic	X	X
Research – Clinical		X
Grants & Contracts	X	X
IRS	X	X
Intercollegiate Athletics	X	
Privacy of Information	X	X
Student Financial Aid	X	X
Gift Restrictions	X	X
Information Resources	X	X
Safeguarding Assets	X	X

APPENDIX F
CONFERENCE PRESENTERS'
BIOGRAPHICAL SKETCHES

Conference Host

Urton Anderson, CIA, CCSA
The University of Texas at Austin

Urton Anderson is Clark W. Thompson, Jr. Professor in Accounting Education and the Associate Dean for Undergraduate Programs at the McCombs School of Business, The University of Texas at Austin. He joined the Department of Accounting in 1984, teaching auditing and managerial accounting. Urton received his Ph.D. from The University of Minnesota in 1985. He is a past recipient of a KPMG Peat Marwick Foundation Research Fellowship and a KPMG Peat Marwick Foundation Faculty Fellowship.

Urton's research has addressed various issues in internal and external auditing. He has written one book, *Quality Assurance for Internal Auditing*, as well as papers published in a variety of scholarly and professional journals. Professor Anderson is a Certified Internal Auditor and from 1994 to 1999 served on the Board of Regents for The Institute of Internal Auditors. In 1999 he was appointed a member of the Internal Auditing Standards Board. He served on the CCSA Steering Committee that developed the professional examination for Control Self-assessment. Currently he serves on the CGAP Steering Committee for the new professional examination in governmental auditing. In 1997 he was named Leon R. Radde Educator of the Year Award by The Institute of Internal Auditors. Professor Anderson is also the co-editor of the quarterly journal *Internal Auditing*.

Higher Education Compliance Pioneers

Steven M. Jung, Ph.D., CIA
Qualifications:
- Fifteen years of service with the Stanford University Internal Audit Department, including Director of Internal Audit since November 1995. I have primary responsibility for:
  - managing all internal audit activities at Stanford University, Stanford Management Company, and Stanford Linear Accelerator Center, including interactions with the Stanford University Board of Trustees Committee on Audit and Senior Management. Recently assumed responsibility for all internal audit functions at Stanford Hospital and Clinics and Lucile Salter Packard Children's Hospital at Stanford.

The Institute of Internal Auditors Research Foundation

- managing all administrative functions of the department (12 professional and two support staff).
- overseeing interactions with all external auditors on campus, including the Defense Contract Audit Agency (DCAA) and PricewaterhouseCoopers LLP (PwC).

• Seventeen years of progressively greater responsibility as a project director, principal investigator, Group Director, and Institute Director at the American Institutes for Research (AIR), a non-profit educational research and behavioral science consulting firm, in Washington, Palo Alto, and Bangkok, Thailand.

Accomplishments at Stanford University:

• Assumed overall responsibility for Stanford's successful Y2K Readiness Program.

• Participated in numerous business process improvement initiatives, including the Executive Steering Committee and Business Council for the University's new Oracle Core Financial System and the Steering Committees for the Property Management Improvement Process and E-Commerce initiatives. Continue to serve on the University Management Committee for all system improvement projects underway at Stanford.

• As Audit Director and Audit Liaison Officer, assisted in the development of improved relations with government auditors on campus.

• In 1986, developed the University's first comprehensive Operating Unit Compliance Audit Program, covering 30+ areas of compliance with government and university policies, and placed this program on the Web, where it is accessible by all faculty and staff as a self-study tool and by internal auditors at other universities, many of whom have adapted it to their own use.

Professional Experience:

Director of Internal Audit, Interim Director, Audit Manager, Managing Auditor, and Associate Managing Auditor, Stanford University Internal Audit Department, 1986-present.

Principal Research Scientist (principal investigator for sponsored research and program evaluation projects with total budgets in excess of $5 million) and Group and Institute Director (management responsibility for staff of 30+ FTE), American Institutes for Research (AIR), Palo Alto, California, and Bangkok, Thailand, 1969-1986.

Education:
Ph.D., Arizona State University, Educational Psychology (Research and Assessment Methods), 1969.
M.A., University of New Mexico, Guidance and Counseling, 1967.
B.S., University of New Mexico, Psychology, 1965.
Professional training programs including: Institute of Internal Auditors course on internal audit quality assurance for external quality assurance peer review, KPMG course on Educational Cost Accounting Standards, NACUBO course on grant and contract accounting, AICPA course on OMB Circular A-133.
Passed all four parts of the Certified Internal Auditor (CIA) examination in first sitting, November 1991.

Affiliations and Service:
Association of College and University Auditors. Chair, Best Practices Committee and immediate past Chair, Government Affairs Committee. In the latter capacity, attended all meetings of the Council on Governmental Relations (COGR) as a member of its Costing Policies Committee, and continue to serve on that Committee as a representative of Stanford University.
The Institute of Internal Auditors. Current Governor, past Treasurer, Second and First Vice President, San Jose Area Chapter.

Awards:
Recipient of Member Excellence Award, Association of College and University Auditors, Montreal, September 2000.

Professional Presentations:
Moderator, Implementing an Effective Compliance Auditing Function, Panel Discussion at 44th Annual Conference, Association of College and University Auditors, Montreal, September 2000.
Presenter, Compliance with OMB Circular A-21 and Cost Accounting Standards, Workshop at 42nd and 43rd Annual Conferences, Association of College and University Auditors, Keystone, Colorado, and St. Louis, Missouri, September 1998 and 1999.
List of over 30 other professional presentations available on request.

Publications:
Jung, Steve and Frank Topper. Risk and Control Self-assessment: The Next Plateau. College and University Auditor, August, 2000.
Topper, Frank, and Steve Jung. Control Self-assessment: Panacea or Useful Tool? College and University Auditor, August 1997.
List of over 50 other professional publications available on request.

Odell Guyton, Esquire

Odell Guyton, Esquire, is the Corporate Compliance Officer for the University of Pennsylvania and the University of Pennsylvania Health System. Mr. Guyton possesses many years of complex litigation and investigative experience in the areas of "white collar" criminal defense, fraud and abuse, tax, money laundering, RICO, and qui tam litigation. In addition, Mr. Guyton has extensive experience in the areas of corporate compliance, corporate internal investigations, legal audit, federal and state grand jury representation and federal sentencing guidelines. Previous to employment at the University of Pennsylvania, Mr. Guyton was engaged in the private practice of law. Mr. Guyton has served in the United States Attorney's Office and the Philadelphia District Attorney's Office. He also serves on several governing boards, including the Board of the health Care Compliance Association. He has authored several articles and received numerous awards, honors, and recognition for his service. Mr. Guyton speaks nationally on the issues of preventative law and corporate compliance. He is currently a candidate for a master's degree in Bioethics at the University of Pennsylvania. He received his Juris Doctor degree from the American University, Washington College of Law, and earned his Bachelor of Arts degree from Moravian College, Bethlehem, Pennsylvania.

Charles G. Chaffin

Charles G. Chaffin has been the Director of Audits for The University of Texas System since 1991 and the System-wide Compliance Officer since 2000. He is responsible for the development and execution of the risk-based system-wide audit plan for 15 components. With six health components and nine academic components employing 75,000 administrators, faculty, and staff with over 150,000 students, the System is one of the largest in the world. During his tenure at UT System, Charlie has overseen the development of the Internal Control Action Plan that ensures accurate financial reporting; the implementation of the Control Self-assessment Process system-wide, and the development and implementation of the Action Plan to Ensure Institutional Compliance. Prior to joining UT System, Charlie was an audit partner with Deloitte & Touche in Houston, specializing in government and education. He is a CPA and CIA

The University of Texas System Executive Management

R. D. (Dan) Burck
CHANCELLOR
Dan Burck was appointed Chancellor of The University of Texas System on December 6, 2000, a position he had held on an interim basis since June. He graduated from The University of Texas at Austin in 1956 with a Bachelor of Business Administration degree, and he attended the South Texas School of Law in Houston. Mr. Burck joined the U. T. System as Vice Chancellor for Business Affairs in 1988 and was named Executive Vice Chancellor for Business Affairs in 1992. At

the U. T. System, his responsibilities have included: finance; business operations, budget, and information resources; human resources; facilities planning and construction; employee group insurance; real estate; and West Texas operations. Mr. Burck established the System's program for increasing purchases from historically under-utilized businesses; has administered a System-wide cost-saving program; and was the first System-wide compliance officer. He came to the U. T. System after a successful 33-year career in private business. Mr. Burck worked for Getty Oil Co. from 1955-1984, and part of his responsibilities were managing the company's worldwide holdings, which included 13 subsidiary companies in fields as diverse as real estate, agriculture, television, forest products, and construction. He was also involved in the creation and early operation of ESPN, the cable TV sports network, serving as a vice president and a director. From 1984-1988, Mr. Burck was president and director of Block Watne Texas, Inc., a builder of residential housing. Mr. Burck is currently a member of the board of directors for Adorno/Rogers Technology, Inc., enerSource Solutions, Inc., and *infiNET* Solutions. He also serves on the Executive Committee of the Council of Public Universities and Chancellors. He has been a member of the board of the Texas Department of Information Resources, the board of directors of the Texas Life, Accident, Health, and Hospital Service Insurance Guaranty Association, the Formula Advisory Committee of the Texas Higher Education Coordinating Board, and the Advisory Council of the U. T. Austin College of Natural Sciences. Mr. Burck is also a former director of the National Conference of Christians and Jews, a former member of the executive committee of the Greater Austin/San Antonio Corridor Council, and a former member of the board of directors of the American Cancer Society.

James C. Guckian, M.D.
VICE CHANCELLOR FOR HEALTH AFFAIRS
Dr. Guckian has been Vice Chancellor for Health Affairs since 1997. He received his BA degree from The University of Texas at Austin, in 1960, graduating with highest honors and Phi Beta Kappa. He received his M.D. degree in 1962 from The University of Texas Medical Branch at Galveston, also graduating with highest honors and Alpha Omega Alpha. He received his internal medicine and infectious diseases training at The University of Texas Medical Branch at Galveston, where he joined the faculty in 1967. His role was fairly equally divided among research, teaching, administration of departmental and educational activities, and patient care. He was promoted to Professor of Internal Medicine and Microbiology in 1979. He directed undergraduate education in the Department of Medicine and was the principal investigator on National Institutes of Health research grants. He received a number of teaching awards from 1971-1985. He authored numerous articles in refereed journals and served on a special task force of the National Board of Medical Examiners on the evaluation of clinical skills. Dr. Guckian is a Diplomate of the American Board of Internal Medicine and Infectious Diseases. Dr. Guckian held the position of Chairman ad Interim of the Department of Medicine for almost two years in 1984-1985. In September 1985, Dr. Guckian was appointed Vice President for Medical Professional Affairs and Medical Director

of the newly created faculty group practice plan for The University of Texas Medical Branch at Galveston.   In April 1988, Dr. Guckian, was appointed as Executive Associate for Health Policy and Planning in The University of Texas System Administration in Austin. His major charge was to develop and implement a statewide managed health care plan for the more than 60,000 employees of The University of Texas System. He served as the U. T. System Employee Group Insurance Program Administrator from 1990 to 1993.   In December 1993, he relinquished management of the employee health plan to become full-time in the U. T. System Office of Health Affairs and was appointed Vice Chancellor for Health Affairs in 1997. He is responsible for providing recommendations and advice to the Chancellor and Executive Vice Chancellor for Health Affairs on national and state health policy and legislation and on opportunities and initiatives that impact health education and health care delivery in the six U. T. System health institutions. He has played a major role in legislative affairs affecting medical education and medical practice in Texas. He has chaired a number of U. T. System Committees and Task Forces, and is Chairman of the Board of Directors of the joint U. T. System-Texas Tech Health Sciences Center health maintenance organization, Texas Universities Health Plan.

Dr. Guckian was elected a Fellow of the American College of Physicians in 1971, and was elected to the prestigious Mastership of the American College of Physicians in 2000.

Kerry L. Kennedy
EXECUTIVE VICE CHANCELLOR FOR BUSINESS AFFAIRS
Current position:
Executive Vice Chancellor for Business Affairs, The University of Texas System
Previous positions:
Assistant Vice Chancellor and Controller, The University of Texas System
Compliance Accomplishments:
Compliance Officer, U. T. System Administration (January 1998 through June 2000)
Publication:
The Right Stuff - the compliance guide for U. T. System Administration Employees (published Fall 1999)

The University of Texas System Components' Executive Management

Leon J. Leach
EXECUTIVE VICE PRESIDENT
The University Of Texas M .D Anderson Cancer Center
Mr. Leon Leach is the Executive Vice President at The University of Texas M. D. Anderson Cancer Center and serves as the Chairman of the Board of the M. D. Anderson Outreach Corporation.

Mr. Leach came to M. D. Anderson from Cornerstone Physicians Corporation where he held the position of Executive Vice President and Chief Financial Officer of Cornerstone Physicians Corporation in Irvine, California. Previously, he has held the positions of Senior Vice President and Chief Financial Officer with CareAmerica Health Plans Inc., a $600 million in revenue HMO and health care company in Southern California. Prior to that Mr. Leach was the Executive Vice President and Chief Financial Officer of Candle SubAcute Services Inc. also in Southern California. Candle was the largest privately held manager of subacute facilities in California until its sale to Vencor Hospitals; a large New York Stock Exchange traded hospital company.

Mr. Leach spent 25 years in various leadership positions at The Prudential Insurance Company of America, serving as Senior Vice President of the Prudential Health Care Plan (PruCare), and subsequently serving as Senior Vice President and Chief Financial Officer of The Prudential Real Estate Affiliates. He was instrumental in the foundation and start up of 18 HMOs through out the southeast and eastern United States while with Prudential.

Leon is married to Tensel Marie Leach. They reside in Houston, Texas with their youngest son Monte. Their two older sons, Bill and Dave, reside in Southern California. Mr. Leach holds a Master of Business Administration degree from Widener University and a Bachelor of Science degree from Rutgers University.

Ricardo Romo
PRESIDENT
The University of Texas at San Antonio
Ricardo Romo became the fifth president of the University of Texas at San Antonio in May 1999. Raised in San Antonio, he graduated from Fox Tech High School on the city's West Side and attended the University of Texas at Austin on a track scholarship, where he earned a Bachelor of Science degree in history. He was the first Texan to run a mile in less than four minutes, and his UT Austin record still stands. Romo holds a master's degree in history from Loyola Marymount University in Los Angeles and a doctorate in history from the University of California at Los Angeles. He began his university teaching career at California State University at Northridge then taught at UC San Diego. In 1980, Romo returned to his undergraduate institution, UT Austin, to teach history. Before he assumed the UTSA presidency, he served as vice provost for undergraduate education at UT Austin.

Romo earned national respect as an urban historian, and he is best known for his 1983 book, *East Los Angeles: History of a Barrio*. The book, which is now in its eighth printing, details the growth of the largest Mexican American community in the United States and describes its contribution to Southern California's early 20th century development. From 1987 to 1993, Romo directed the Texas office of the Tomás Rivera Center, housed at Trinity University in San Antonio. The Center is a national organization that evaluates the impact of governmental policies on Latinos. Romo met his wife, Harriett, while the two were students at UT Austin, where she earned an undergraduate degree in elementary education. She holds a doctorate in sociology and is an associate professor in social and policy sciences at UTSA. She also works with the National Head Start Family Service Center in San Marcos.

The Romo's son, Carlos, graduated from Stanford University. Their daughter, Anadelia, is a doctoral candidate at Harvard University.

Robert E. Witt
PRESIDENT
The University of Texas at Arlington
Robert E. Witt became President of The University of Texas at Arlington on June 1, 1995. Prior to that time, beginning in April 1986, Dr. Witt was Dean of the College and Graduate School of Business at The University of Texas at Austin and holds the Centennial Chair in Business Education Leadership. Also at UT Austin, before becoming Dean, he was Acting Dean, Associate Dean for Academic Affairs and Chairman of the Department of Marketing Administration. President Witt received his B. A. in Economics from Bates College, his MBA from Tuck School at Dartmouth College, and his Ph.D. from Penn State. He is the author of numerous research articles and has been an active member of the American Marketing Association. He currently serves on the Board of Directors of Arlington Chamber of Commerce, and is a Director of Arlington's Chase Bank.

The University of Texas System Institutional Compliance Officers

Sharron Devere
The University of Texas Health Science Center at Houston
Sharron Devere is the Assistant Vice President and Chief Compliance Officer at the The University of Texas Health Science Center at Houston. Ms. Devere has served as the chief compliance officer in the Office of Institutional Compliance since its inception two and one-half years ago. Ms. Devere has been with the university for 13 years. She previously spent over 10 years in the Internal Audit Department in various audit positions including audit manager and interim director. Ms. Devere has been responsible for developing and implementing the university-wide compliance program. She developed a self-assessment survey to evaluate the effectiveness of the university's compliance program to instill compliance awareness and its impact on its employees. She has presented this tool at one of the recent Association of Colleges and University Auditors conference as well as to the UT System-wide Compliance Committee. Ms. Devere is a certified public accountant and certified fraud examiner. She holds a Master of Science in Accountancy from The University of Houston. She is a member of the American Institute of Certified Accountants and the AAMC Compliance Officers' Forum.

Carrie King, J. D.
The University of Texas M.D. Anderson Cancer Center
Ms. King currently serves as the Chief Compliance Officer for The University of Texas M. D. Anderson Cancer Center. During her career she has held positions as Legal Counsel for The University of Texas Office of General Counsel, In-House Counsel for a Houston-based Insurance Company and as a Briefing Attorney for the U. S. Department of Health and Human Services. Ms. King currently serves on the UT System System-wide Compliance Committee. She has made numerous presentations to medical, nursing, and medical office staff. Additionally, she has been a Texas Medical Association keynote speaker.

Gayle Knight
The University of Texas Health Science Center at San Antonio
Gayle Knight is the Assistant Vice President for Institutional Compliance/Institutional Compliance Officer for The University of Texas Health Science Center at San Antonio. Ms. Knight has been responsible for developing and implementing a compliance program for the University. She has been with the institution for over twelve years and previously was the Director of Internal Audit.

She has conducted a peer review of The University of Texas System Compliance Program, including the System-wide Compliance Program. Also, she has conducted numerous peer reviews of internal audit departments.

Ms. Knight previously worked as a manager for one of the large public accounting firms for approximately six years. She is a certified public accountant and has a Bachelor of Business Administration degree from The University of Texas at San Antonio. She is a member of the American Institute of Certified Accountants and the AAMC Compliance Officers' Forum

David R. Larson
The University of Texas at San Antonio
Current position:
Vice President of Business Affairs at The University of Texas San Antonio (UTSA)
Previous positions:
Vice President for Business and Finance at Clemson University
Vice Chancellor for Administration and Finance at The University of Tennessee at Chattanooga
Vice Chancellor for Business and Finance at The University of Tennessee at Chattanooga
Accomplishments:
Implemented Continuous Improvement Program for business operations to improve services to the campus community

Implemented new organizational paradigm for Information Technology based on outcomes identified by the institutions Learning Vision Project

Established Compliance Program at UTSA

Developed and implemented operational systems for UTSA's new campus in downtown San Antonio

John A. Roan

The University of Texas Southwestern Medical Center at Dallas

Current position:

Executive Vice President for Business Affairs, The University of Texas Southwestern Medical Center at Dallas

Previous positions:

Senior Vice President for Business Affairs, The University of Texas Southwestern Medical Center at Dallas

Vice President for Business Affairs, The University of Texas Southwestern Medical Center at Dallas

Assistant Vice Chancellor for Finance, The University of Texas System

Compliance Accomplishments:

Member of The University of Texas System System-wide Compliance Committee

Scott Scarborough, CPA, CIA, CISA

The University of Texas at Tyler

Current position:

Vice President for Business Affairs and Compliance Officer at The University of Texas at Tyler

Previous positions:

Audit Manager at The University of Texas System Audit Office

Assistant Director of The University of Texas System Employee Group Insurance Program

Audit Supervisor at Coopers & Lybrand

Audit Supervisor at KPMG Peat Marwick

Compliance Accomplishments:

Member of the System-wide Compliance Committee

The University of Texas System and Component Compliance Specialist

Nancy M. Gast
The University of Texas Medical Branch at Galveston
Current position:
Executive Director of Institutional Compliance and Cost Reimbursements University of Texas
Medical Branch at Galveston
Previous positions:
Director of Cost Reimbursements ,University of Texas Medical Branch at Galveston Director of
Admitting and Patient Accounts, University of Texas Medical Branch at Galveston
Compliance Accomplishments:
AAMC Fraud & Abuse Task Force (Currently serving)
U.T. System Compliance Training Delivery Subcommittee – Chairperson
U.T. System Research Compliance Committee
U.T. System Compliance Training Core Curriculum Subcommittee
Speaker – Subject: Compliance Programs:
Texas Association of College & University Business Officers
Southeast Cost Accounting Conference (SECA)
Southern Association of College & University Business Officers (March, 2001)

Paul Henry
The University of Texas System Office of Health Affairs
Current position:
Special Assistant for Management and Compliance for The University of Texas System Office of
Health Affairs
Previous positions:
Audit Manager for The University of Texas System Audit Office
Compliance Accomplishments:
Responsible for oversight of the compliance programs at the UT System Health Components
Responsible for organizing the Medical Billing and Research Compliance Workgroups and HIPAA
Coordinators meetings

John W. Sparks, M.D.
The University of Texas Health Science Center at Houston
Current position:
Compliance Office, The University of Texas Health Science Center at Houston Medical School
Professor and Chair, Department of Pediatrics, The University of Texas Health Science Center at Houston Medical School
Compliance accomplishments:
Member of The University of Texas System-wide Compliance Committee

Angela R. Charboneau Wishon, J.D
The University of Texas Medical Branch at Galveston
Current position:
Director, Research Facilitation & Compliance The University of Texas Medical Branch at Galveston
Previous position:
Legal Office Manager
Office of Vice Chancellor and General Counsel Washington University
Accomplishments:
Committees:
Co-Chair of the Monitoring Subcommittee for NACUBO's Working Group on University Compliance
Member of UT System Research Compliance Committee
Member of UTMB's Conflict of Interest Committee
Presentations:
Research Audit Management –
NCURA Region 5 Spring Meeting (4/00)
TACUA Annual Meeting (6/00)
TASUA Meeting (7/00)
Research Compliance Monitoring - AAMC/NACUBO Meeting (6/00)
Best Practices in Clinical Monitoring – COGR/NACUBO Meeting (10/00)
Ensuring Human Subjects Protection
UT System Compliance Officers & Committee Meetings (11/00)
UTMB Conference (11/00)
Crisis Management in Dealing with Auditors – NCURA Region 5 Spring Meeting – (4/01)
Research Financial Management – NACUBO (5/01)
Publications:
"A Tricky Business: Assessing Risks from an Institutional Perspective," Clinical Researcher, Cheryl Chanaud, Ph.D., Ann Smith and Angela Wishon, J.D., February 2001

The University of Texas System-wide High Risk Work Group Representatives

Carleen A. Brunelli, Ph.D., M.B.A.
Clinical Research High Risk Work Group
Current Position:
Chief Research and Regulatory Affairs Officer
The University of Texas M. D. Anderson Cancer Center
Previous positions:
Executive Director, Office of Research Administration, Univ. of Texas, M.D. Anderson Cancer Center
Administrative Director, Office of Protocol Research, Univ. of Texas, M.D. Anderson Cancer Center
Visiting Scientist, Thoracic and Cardiovascular Surgery, Univ. of Texas, M. D. Anderson Cancer Center
Project Manager, Introgen Therapeutics, Inc. Houston, TX
Research Laboratory Coordinator, Molecular Biology and Biochemistry, Brown University, Providence, R.I.
Compliance Accomplishments:
Publications:
Buzdar A U, Brunelli C A Zwelling L A. Protecting Human Subjects from Risk in the Performance of Clinical Research and the Informed Consent Process. Progress in Anti-Cancer Chemotherapy. 7-15, 1999
Membership Information:
University of Texas M. D. Anderson Cancer Center Institutional Compliance Committee
University of Texas System System-wide Compliance Committee
Co-Chair, University of Texas System High Risk Research Committee
Conference Information:
Annual CCOP mtg., September 2000, Univ. of Texas, M. D. Anderson Cancer Center, Invited Speaker

Lynn Hickey
Intercollegiate Athletics High Risk Work Group
The University Of Texas At San Antonio Athletic Director
Lynn Hickey began a new chapter in her athletic administration career on August 27, 1999, when she was named the athletic director at The University of Texas at San Antonio. In becoming the fourth athletic director in UTSA history, Hickey assumes the lead athletic role in one of the youngest NCAA Division I universities in the country; UTSA began athletic competition in 1981. Today, the program includes 14 sports, seven for men and seven for women. UTSA has played host to some of America's most prestigious collegiate sporting events that include the 1997 Men's Basketball Midwest Regional, 1998 Men's Basketball Final Four and the 1998 Men's Golf Central

Regional. Future events to be hosted by UTSA include the 2001 Men's Basketball Midwest Regional, 2002 Women's Basketball Final Four, 2003 Men's Basketball South Regional and the 2004 Men's Basketball Final Four. Hickey came to San Antonio from Texas A & M University, where she had served as senior associate athletic director/senior woman administrator since 1994. At Texas A & M, her responsibilities included event management and marketing and promotions for 16 of the university's 19 Division I sports programs. She also has represented the Big Twelve Conference as a member of the NCAA Championship Cabinet. From 1984 to 1994, Hickey served as head women's basketball coach for Texas A & M. She directed the 1993-94 Lady Aggie basketball team to the Sweet Sixteen at the NCAA Tournament, becoming the lowest seeded team to ever reach that milestone. Texas A & M finished the year ranked No. 19 in the CNN/USA Top 25 Poll. Following the season she relinquished her coaching duties to accept the promotion to senior associate athletic director. She finished her coaching career with an overall mark of 279-167 in 15 years of collegiate coaching. She came to A & M from Kansas State University, where she was the head women's basketball coach from 1979 to 1984, and led the Wildcats to at least 23 wins a season and five consecutive NCAA Tournament berths. A native of Welch, Okla., she graduated summa cum laude from Ouachita Baptist University with a bachelor of science degree in education and was an All-American for OBU's nationally ranked basketball team and a member of the USA National Team in 1973. She and her husband, Bill Hickey, have one daughter, Lauren Nicole.

Deiter A. Lehnortt
Medical Billing High Risk Work Group
Current position:
Director, Office of Billing Compliance
The University of Texas Southwestern Medical Center at Dallas
Previous positions:
Assistant Director, Government Affairs Department, American College of Emergency Physicians
Director, Physician Reimbursement Department, American College of Emergency Physicians
Vice President, Health Policy and Payer Relations Medical Management Resources, Inc.
Executive Director, MedTrust Healthcare Services Company, Inc
Compliance Accomplishments:
Member - UT Southwestern Medical Center at Dallas Institutional Compliance Committee.
<u>Publications</u>:
Contributing author – *Emergency Department Management: Principles and Applications*, Mosby, 1997.
Editorial Board member – *Procedure Coding for Emergency Medicine: An Educational Manual*, American College of Emergency Physicians, 1989 (First Edition) and 1993 (Second Edition).

Dr. Richard Padilla
Student Financial Aid High Risk Work Group
Current position:
Vice President for Student Affairs - The University of Texas at El Paso
Previous positions:
Dean of Student Affairs at The University of Houston
Associate Dean of Students at The University of Houston
Compliance Accomplishments:
Member of The University of Texas System System-wide Compliance Committee
Representative of students in the area of Student Financial Aid
President of the Council of Student Affairs Vice Presidents

Anthony T. Ramirez
Human Resources High Risk Work Group
Current position:
Director of Human Resources, The University of Texas Health Science Center San Antonio
Previous position:
Assistant Director of Human Resources, The University of Texas Health Science Center San Antonio
Compliance Accomplishments:
Serves on the Institutional Compliance Committee and the System-wide Compliance Committee.

Juan M. Sanchez
Basic Research High Risk Work Group
Current position:
Vice President for Research, UT Austin
Previous position:
Research Associate, Univ. of California, Los Angeles, CA 1977-79
Visiting Professor, Univ. of Sao Paulo, Sao Carlos, Brazil 1979
Research Associate and Lecturer, Univ. of California, Berkeley, CA 1980-81
Asst. Professor 1981-85, Assoc. Professor 1985-87, Professor 1987-89 Columbia University, New York, NY
Professor, The University of Texas, Austin, TX 1989-present
Compliance Accomplishments:
Member, Board of Directors, Austin Software Council and Texas Society for Biological Research; Associate Editor, Journal of Phase Equilibria; Member, Acta Metallurgica/Hume-Rothery Award Committee of the Minerals, Metals, and Materials Society; past Chairman of the Committee on Alloy Phases; Member, Council of the Structural Materials Division and of the Steering Committee of the Electronics, Magnetic and Photonic Materials Division; Member, Supercomputer Simu-

lation Committee of the National Materials Advisory Board, National Research Council. Member, Board of Trustees, Association of Western Universities.

Dr. Sanchez is a Member of Sigma Xi Research Society, Metallurgical Society, Materials Research Society, American Physical Society, and Japan Institute of Metals.

Kim A. Smith
Environmental Health & Safety High Risk Work Group
Current position:
Director Of Safety, Health and Environmental Services and Safety Officer, The University of Texas Health Center at Tyler, Texas
Previous positions:
Environmental and Safety Consultant and Owner of Engineering and Safety Consultants, Tyler, Texas
Compliance Accomplishments:
Keynote speaker at the 2000 National Conference of The Joint Commission of Accredited Hospital Organization on computer based training implementation
Member of UTHCT Compliance Committee
Chairman-Elect of UT System Environmental Advisory Committee
Co-author and developer of The Training Post, a computer based training program implemented within the UT System

The University of Texas Component Internal Audit Directors

J. Michael Peppers
The University of Texas Medical Branch at Galveston
J. Michael Peppers is the Director of Audit Services for The University of Texas Medical Branch at Galveston. UTMB leads the top 10 University Hospital Consortium facilities nationwide in the number of inpatient admissions and clinic visits and has the second-highest number of hospital beds. He has responsibility for all aspects of the University's internal auditing, assurance, advising, and investigation activities. He reports to the president of the institution and leads a staff of sixteen professionals. Mr. Peppers' previous experience includes nine years as the chief audit executive at the University of South Florida and four years in public accounting.

Mr. Peppers is a Certified Internal Auditor (CIA) and Certified Public Accountant (CPA) and has bachelor's and master's degrees in Accountancy. He is the Vice-President/President-Elect of the Association of College and University Auditors and previously served as an elected board member to that organization for three years. He is a Past President of the Florida West Coast Chapter of The Institute of Internal Auditors (IIA). He is currently a member of the Board of Governors of the Houston Chapter of the IIA. Mr. Peppers is an active public speaker on internal audit related topics. He is a Distinguished Faculty Member in The IIA's Volunteer Faculty program and leads courses each year at IIA seminars around the country.

APPENDIX G
STEPS FOR IMPLEMENTING AN
EFFECTIVE COMPLIANCE PROGRAM

1. The governance function and/or the chief executive officer must **recognize the need for an institutional compliance program.** (Chapter 1)

2. The chief executive officer **appoints an ad hoc committee representing all elements of the institutional community to develop an action plan** for implementation and operation of the compliance program. (Chapters 2 and 3)

3. The chief executive officer **appoints an institutional compliance officer and an institutional compliance committee.** (Chapter 5)

4. The chief executive officer and the institutional compliance officer **decide on the structure of the compliance function.** (Chapter 5)

5. The compliance officer, as required by the structure of the compliance function, **appoints a compliance coordinator and other compliance function staff.** (Chapter 5)

6. The compliance officer and the compliance committee **prepare a standards of conduct guide.** (Chapter 6)

7. The compliance officer **establishes a confidential reporting mechanism for employees to use to anonymously report potential instances of noncompliance.** (Chapter 10)

8. The compliance officer and the compliance committee **establish the general compliance training program content based upon the standards of conduct guide.** (Chapter 6)

9. The compliance officer and the compliance committee **develop a general compliance training plan**, including appropriate training delivery and testing methodologies. (Chapter 6)

10. The compliance officer, the compliance committee, and the compliance function **facilitate a compliance risk assessment of the institution, including the identification of the institution's "A" risks.** (Chapter 7)

11. The compliance committee and the compliance officer may **appoint a compliance committee working group representing all of the institution's "A" risk areas** to assist the compliance committee in performing specific tasks. (Chapter 5)

12. The compliance officer **ensures that each institution "A" risk has a risk management design** that includes (1) a single responsible party, (2) an appropriate monitoring plan, (3) an appropriate specialized training plan, and a reporting plan. (Chapter 8)

13. The compliance officer and the compliance committee, with input from the governance function and the chief executive officer, **establish a compliance assurance plan for the institution to ensure that management of the institution's "A" risks is being performed as designed.** (Chapter 9)

14. The compliance officer **reports instances of potential and/or actual noncompliance to the chief executive officer as required.** (Chapter 5)

15. Operating management **deals with instances of noncompliance as specified in the policies and procedures that govern each process in the institution.** (Chapter 11).

16. The compliance officer **makes periodic reports to the chief executive officer on the activities of the compliance program.** (Chapter 5)

17. The compliance officer and the compliance committee **perform an annual self-assessment of the compliance program and, when needed, arrange for an external peer review of the compliance program.** (Chapter 12)

18. The compliance officer and the compliance committee **prepare an action plan to implement improvements to the compliance program identified in the self-assessment and/or the external peer review.** (Chapter 12)

APPENDIX H
THE UNIVERSITY OF TEXAS SYSTEM INSTITUTIONAL COMPLIANCE STANDARDS OF CONDUCT GUIDE

Purpose

The purpose of the *Standards of Conduct Guide ("Guide")* is to emphasize the necessity for and the responsibility of all employees* of The University of Texas System ("U.T. System") to be aware of and perform their duties and responsibilities in compliance with all applicable provisions of federal and state laws, regulations, and policies; the <u>Policies</u> and the <u>Rules and Regulations</u> of the Board of Regents of the U.T. System; and the policies and rules and regulations of the U.T. System component institution at which they are employed. This *Guide* is an outline of various laws, policies, rules and regulations that govern the conduct of employees of the U.T. System. Although the *Guide* addresses a number of specific laws, policies, rules and regulations, it is not intended to be a comprehensive list of legal and ethical standards, but provides employees of the U.T. System with information about and source references for the laws, policies, rules, and regulations that govern their conduct. It also represents an educational tool and information directory to be used by the U.T. System Compliance Risk Management Program for training employees of the U.T. System regarding the conduct required of them. Specific ethical or compliance questions of employees should be directed to the U.T. System Administration's or the component institution's Ethics Officer or Compliance Officer.

Compliance Risk Management Program

The U.T. System Compliance Program ("Program") is intended to demonstrate in the clearest possible terms the absolute commitment of the U.T. System to the highest standards of ethics and compliance with all applicable laws, policies, rules and regulations. Program direction is provided by a System-wide Compliance Committee representing all major compliance areas. The U.T. System Compliance Officer, Mr. R. D. Burck, Executive Vice Chancellor for Business Affairs, is responsible for the execution of the Program. Each U.T. System component institution has a Compliance Officer and a Compliance Committee.

---

*The term "employees of The University of Texas System ("U.T. System")" includes all officers, administrators, faculty, classified and non-classified staff, and professional personnel employed by the U.T. System Administration and component institutions of the U.T. System.

Compliance issues should be addressed through normal administrative channels. However, a reporting procedure has been established at U.T. System Administration and each of the component institutions as a way for employees to report instances of suspected non-compliance outside the normal chain of command in a manner that preserves confidentiality to the extent allowed by law. Information about the reporting procedure may be addressed to the Compliance Officer of the component institution, or if a U.T. System employee, to the System Compliance Officer.

Standards of Conduct

1. **Ethical Standards.** The State of Texas and the Board of Regents of The University of Texas System have defined certain ethical standards that apply to employees of the U.T. System. The most complete and current source of information on ethical standards is the U. T. System Office of General Counsel ("OGC") Web page, accessible via the Internet at http://www.utsystem.edu/OGC/. Included in this Web site is the U.T. System's Ethics Policy, which is part of the Regents' Rules and Regulations. The Office of General Counsel has also published a *Standards of Conduct Digest* that provides excerpts from principal state law, Ethics Advisory Opinions, Regents' Rules and Regulations, and System policies involving standards for officers and employees.

   Ethical behavior is expected of every employee of the U.T. System. Management personnel at every level are expected to set an ethical "tone at the top" and to be role models for ethical behavior in their departments. They should create a departmental culture that promotes the highest standards of ethics and encourages everyone in the department to voice concerns when unethical behavior or incidents of non-compliance with applicable laws, policies, rules or regulations arise. Each employee has a personal obligation to report any activity that appears to violate such laws, policies, rules and regulations.

2. **Contacts with the media, government and outside investigators.** The U.T. System expects to cooperate in government investigations of the U.T. System, the component institutions, or employees with due consideration given to the legal rights of the U.T. System, the component institution and employees of the U.T. System. If a subpoena, other legal document, or inquiry from an external governmental agency related to institution business is received by an employee of the U.T. System, whether at home or in the workplace, such employee is obligated to notify their supervisor immediately. If contacted at home by an external governmental agent, without search warrant or subpoena, concerning business of the U.T. System or a component institution, the employee should request that the agent make such contact at work the next business day, and to immediately contact his or her supervisor.

The Institute of Internal Auditors Research Foundation

The Director of News and Public Information acts as the spokesperson for U.T. System Administration. If an employee of U.T. System is contacted by a member of the media, the media representative should be referred to the Director. Additional information regarding contacts with the media, government and outside investigators can be obtained via the Internet at http://www.utsystem.edu/BPM/32.htm.

3. **Records and Information**
   Confidential Information. Unless specifically exempted from or made confidential by law, all documents generated in the regular course of business by the U.T. System Administration and the component institutions are available to the public under the terms and conditions of the Texas Public Information Act. Generally, documentation that is excepted from disclosure includes certain personnel data, student information, patient information, financial data, strategic plans, marketing strategies, supplier and subcontract information, and proprietary computer software. Written requests for documents under the Texas Public Information Act should be handled pursuant to Business Procedures Memorandum ("BPM") No. 32, accessible via the Internet at http://www.utystem.edu/BPM/32.htm.

   Accuracy of Records. Employees of the U.T. System are required to maintain the integrity and accuracy of business documents and records for which they are responsible. No one may alter or falsify information on any record or document.

   Retention and Disposal of Records. The U.T. System recognizes the need for orderly management and retrieval of all official records and a documented records retention and destruction schedule that is consistent with state and federal laws and regulations. The U.T. System policy for records management may be found at http://www.utsystem.edu/systempolicies/record.htm. Questions about specific record retention requirements should be directed to the Record Retention Officer in the U.T. System Office of Information Resources or to the person responsible for implementing the record retention at the component institution.

4. **Workplace Conduct and Employment Requirements**
   Fraud. The minimization of fraud, waste, and abuse is the responsibility of all employees of the U.T. System. The U.T. System has established a policy regarding internal investigations of suspected defalcation, misappropriation, and other fiscal irregularities. A copy of the U. T. System's "Statement of Operating Policy Pertaining to Dishonest or Fraudulent Activities," Business Procedures Memorandum (BPM) No. 50, may be obtained through the U.T. System Office of Human Resources or the human resources department of the component institution, the U.T. System Administration Ethics Officer or his or her counterpart at the component institution, or via the Internet at http://www.utsystem.edu/BPM/50.htm.

The Institute of Internal Auditors Research Foundation

Equal Employment Opportunities. Under the terms of applicable laws and regulations, the U.T. System and component institutions may not discriminate against employees or applicants for employment on the basis of race, color, national origin, religion, sex, age, veteran status, or disability. Regents' Rules and Regulations, Part Two, Chapter I. Section 6, are accessible via the Internet at http://www.utsystem.edu/regMSWord/tocrrr.htm. A copy of U.T. System Office of Human Resources Policy Number I.150 ("Equal Employment Opportunity and Affirmative Action") may also be accessed via the Internet at http://www.utsystem.edu/OHR/aapolicy.htm or obtained through the U.T. System Office of Human Resources.

Sexual Harassment and Sexual Misconduct: The U.T. System Administration and the component institutions are committed to the principal that the working environment should be free from inappropriate conduct of a sexual nature. Sexual misconduct and sexual harassment are unprofessional behaviors and employees who engage in such conduct will be subject to disciplinary action, including termination. The ethics policy of the U.T. System at Part One, Chapter III, Section 4.8 of the Regents' Rules and Regulations (http://www.utsystem.edu/regMSWord/tocrrr.htm) includes specific provisions regarding sexual harassment and sexual misconduct. A copy of U.T. System Office of Human Resources Policy Number VI.100 ("Sexual Harassment and Sexual Misconduct) may be obtained through the U.T. System's Office of Human Resources.

Overtime Compensation. The federal Fair Labor Standards Act ("FLSA") entitles non-exempt employees of the U.T. System who are required or permitted to work in excess of forty hours in a work week to additional compensation for such excess hours by receiving either compensatory time off or payment for overtime at the rate of time and one-half. Part Two, Chapter V, Section 2.3 of the Regents' Rules and Regulations, accessible via the Internet at http://www.utsystem.edu/regMSWord/tocrrr.htm, provides information pertaining to overtime compensation in accordance with the FLSA. Information pertaining to overtime compensation for U.T. System Administration employees, including the need for prior written approval, is set forth in the U.T. System Office of Human Resources Policy Number II.190 ("Overtime Compensation") accessible through the U.T. System Office of Human Resources.

Family and Medical Leave Act. An employee may request and receive a leave of absence without pay for up to twelve weeks per year for certain family and medical reasons specified by the federal Family and Medical Leave Act of 1993 ("FMLA") and accompanying regulations governing the FMLA. This is a leave program that has specific eligibility requirements and restrictions. More detailed information may be located at Part Two, Chapter V, Section 2.2 of the Regents' Rules and Regulations (http://www.utsystem.edu/regMSWord/tocrrr.htm) and from the U.T. System Office of Human Resources Policy Number VIII.140 ("Family and Medical Leave Act") accessible through the U.T. System Office of Human Resources.

Exempt and Non-Exempt Time Keeping. The Fair Labor Standards Act requires accurate time and leave records for all non-exempt employees of the U.T. System to be maintained. The U.T. System Administration also maintains leave records for exempt employees. Guidelines and procedures to determine positions that qualify for exemption under the FLSA are set forth in U.T. System Office of Human Resources Policy Number II.110 ("Fair Labor Standards Act") accessible through the UT System Office of Human Resources.

Outside Employment. The first responsibility of the faculty and staff is to the U.T. System, and outside professional commitments should not interfere with a faculty or staff member's responsibility to the U.T. System and the component institutions. No member of the faculty or staff shall accept outside employment, temporary or regular, that actually or potentially results in any conflict of interest with or intrudes upon or detracts from the individual's responsibilities to the U.T. System and the component institutions, or to the programs, policies, and objectives of the U.T. System and the component institutions. Consulting and other professional commitments that present this result or the potential for such a result also must be avoided. No full-time employee shall be employed in any outside work or activity or receive from an outside source a regular retainer fee or salary until a description of the nature and extent of the employment has been filed with and approved by the appropriate administrative officials as set forth in the institutional Handbook of Operating Procedures. Regents' Rules and Regulations, Part One, Chapter III, Section 13 specifically addresses the outside employment issue, and it may be obtained via the Internet at http://www.utsystem.edu/ regMSWord/ tocrr.htm.

Financial interests. State laws, court decisions, opinions of the Attorney General, and the policy of the Regents prohibit employees of the U.T. System from having a direct or indirect interest, financial or otherwise, in a corporation or business, engage in a professional activity, or incur an obligation of any nature that is in substantial conflict with or might reasonably tend to influence the discharge of the employee's official duties. Information pertaining to the Regents' policy may be located at the OGC ethics site and via the Internet at http:// www.utsystem.edu/systempolicies/finstmt.htm.

Health and Safety

Workplace health and safety and protection of the environment. All U.T. System employees should perform their duties in compliance with all applicable institutional policies, federal, state and local laws and standards relating to the environment and protection of worker health and safety. You should become familiar with and understand how these laws, standards, and policies apply to your specific job responsibilities and seek advice from your supervisor or the Safety Officer, as needed. Each employee is responsible for advising the employee's supervisor or the Safety Officer of any serious workplace injury or any situation presenting a danger of injury so that timely corrective action may be taken. Information pertaining to the Regents' Policy may be obtained via the Internet at http://www.utsystem.edu/systempolicies/environ2.htm.

Drug and weapon-free workplace. The unlawful manufacture, distribution, possession, or use of a controlled substance in or on any premises or property owned or controlled by the U.T. System ("U.T. property") is prohibited. Any employee found guilty (including a plea of no contest) or has a sentence, fine or other criminal penalty imposed by a court for an offense involving a controlled substance that occurred in or on U.T. property shall report such action to the employee's supervisor or to the Office of Human Resources within five (5) days. An employee who unlawfully manufactures, sells, distributes, possesses or uses a controlled substance on U.T. property, regardless of whether such activity results in the imposition of a penalty under a criminal statute, will be subject to appropriate disciplinary action, including termination, or will be required to participate satisfactorily in an approved drug assistance or rehabilitation program or both. Information pertaining to the Regents' Policy may be obtained via the Internet at http://www.utsystem.edu/systempolicies/drugwork.htm.

Use of U.T. and State of Texas Resources

Contracts and agreements. No employee is authorized to sign a contract or agreement that purports to bind the institution unless that employee has official written delegated authority to do so under the Regents' Rules and Regulations. Do not sign a contract or agreement on behalf of the U.T. System unless you are certain that you have proper authority to execute the document and you take all related actions required under the Regents' Rules and Regulations, Part Two, Chapters 11 & 13, which can be obtained via the Internet at http://www.utystem.edu/regMSWord/tocrr.htm.

Use of state-owned property. An employee may use U.T. property and assets, including personnel time, only for state purposes. As a general rule, the personal use of any U.T. property or asset is prohibited. Incidental personal use of the U.T. System e-mail, a state telephone to make a local telephone call, or the Internet, provided that the use complies with applicable U.T. System policies and does not result in additional cost to the U.T. System, is permissible. Direct any questions you might have about the use of U.T. property to your supervisor. Information regarding the use of state-owned property may be obtained via the Internet at http://www.utsystem.edu/BPM/53.htm.

Computer software. Employees who use software licensed to the U.T. System must abide by applicable software license agreements and may copy licensed software only as permitted by the license. Direct any questions you have about applicable software license agreements to your supervisor or the Office of Information Resources. Information regarding the use of computer software may be obtained via the Internet at http://www.utsystem.edu/BPM/53.htm.

Information: Security and acceptable use. U.T. System information resources may be used only for official state purposes. Every U.T. System employee has a responsibility for maintaining the security and confidentiality of U.T. System's information resources and must comply with information security policies and procedures. An employee may access or disclose confidential and sensitive information only as permitted by contract, state or federal law or regulation, the scope of the employee's employment, or approved U.T. System policy. Information regarding the security and acceptable use of information may be obtained via the Internet at http://www.utsystem.edu/BPM/53.htm.

Computer access, passwords and other confidential information. No employee may knowingly access a computer network or system without the effective consent of the owner or intentionally or knowingly disclose a password, identification code or number, debit card or bank account number, or other confidential information about a computer security system without the consent of the person employing the security system. Information regarding computer access, passwords, and other confidential information may be obtained via the Internet at http://www.utsystem.edu/BPM/53.htm.

Purchasing. No employee may expend U.T. System funds for any purchase unless the person is authorized to make the purchase in accordance with the Regents' Rules and Regulations, Part Two, Chapter 4 (http://www.utsystem.edu/regMSWord/tocrrr.htm), and the purchase is made in accordance with all institutional purchasing procedures, including procedures concerning Historically Underutilized Businesses. Purchases from or sales to an employee of supplies, materials, services, equipment, or property must have the prior approval of the Chancellor or Chief Administrative Officer and the applicable Vice Chancellor, except purchases made at a public auction.

Copyright and Intellectual Property

Photocopying of copyrighted material. Permission must be obtained from the copyright owner to copy copyrighted materials where (a) copying is not fair use, (b) advice of the Office of General Counsel has not been sought, and (c) copying extends beyond the boundaries of the guidelines contained in Appendix I of the Photocopying Copyrighted Materials policy (http://www.utsystem.edu/ogc/systempolicies/copyrite.htm). Most works should be presumed to be copyright protected, unless further information from the copyright holder or express notice reveals that the copyright holder intends the work to be in the public domain.

Intellectual property. The Board of Regents owns the intellectual property created by its students and employees if the intellectual property is created by an employee within the scope of employment; created by an employee on U.T. System time with the use of U.T. System facilities or state financial support; commissioned by U.T. System pursuant to a signed contract; fits within one of the nine categories of works considered works for hire under copyright law; or results from research supported by federal funds or third party sponsorship. An employee must disclose the intellectual property created by the employee to the component institutions' Intellectual Property Advisory Committees well before the employee submits any information about the intellectual property for publication, or makes any public disclosure or even a private disclosure to a commercial entity. Policies regarding intellectual property may be obtained via the Internet at http://www.utsystem.edu/regMSWord/tocrrr.htm (Regents' Rules, Part Two, Chapter 12) and http://www.utsystem.edu/OGC/RegentalPolicies/int-prop.htm (UT System Internet Policy).

5. Political activities and contributions

Political activities. An employee may participate in political activities only if such activities are not conducted during work hours; are in compliance with the Constitution and laws of the State of Texas; do not interfere with the discharge and performance of the employee's duties and responsibilities; do not involve the use of equipment, supplies, or services of U.T. System; do not involve the attempt to coerce students, faculty, or staff to participate in or support the political activity; and do not involve U.T. System in partisan politics. Regents' Rules, Part One, Chapter Three, Sec. 35, regarding political activities, may be obtained via the Internet at http://www.utsystem.edu/systempolicies/politics.htm.

Political contributions. Political contributions from any source of U.T. System funds are prohibited.

6. **Gifts and gratuities.**

Gifts made to influence decisions. An employee must not accept or solicit any gift, favor, or service that might reasonably tend to influence the discharge of the employee's official duties or that the employee knows or should know is being offered with the intent to influence the employee's official conduct. Regents' Rules, Part One, Chapter 1, Sec. 10, regarding gifts and gratuities, may be obtained via the Internet at http://www.utsystem.edu/regMSWord/tocrrr.htm.

Gifts from Persons "Subject to U.T. System Jurisdiction." An employee must not solicit, accept, or agree to accept any benefit from a person the employee knows may have a business relationship with U.T. System, except as permitted under Section 36.10 of the Texas Penal Code. If in doubt, do not accept a benefit offered to you because you are a U.T. System employee. Texas Penal Code, Section 36.08.

Honorarium. An employee must not solicit, accept, or agree to accept an honorarium in consideration for services that the employee should not have been requested to provide but for the employee's official position or duties. Additional information on this issue may be obtained via the Internet at http://www.utsystem.edu/ogc/ethics/guidenew.htm.

APPENDIX I
SAMPLE MONITORING PLAN

Note: This monitoring plan is not a statement of official policy of the institution. It represents an education tool and information directory to be used by the institution's Compliance Risk Management program. The official rules, regulations, and policies of the institution are published in the <u>Policies</u> and <u>Rules and Regulations</u> of the Board of Regents of the institution. This monitoring plan is intended to be a model for risk mitigation and may not be applicable to all situations.

6.3 <u>*Employee Relations Practices: Sexual Harassment*</u>

Summary: Subjecting an employee to any of the several specified forms of behavior that are defined as sexual harassment is an unlawful act that can result in significant liability to the U.T. System.

Legal Basis: Title VII of the Civil Rights Act of 1964, as amended, 42 U.S.C. §2000e et seq.

Enforcement Mechanisms: Internal complaints are addressed by sexual harassment complaint procedures. External complaints are enforced by regulatory agencies and federal and state courts.

Specific Risk: Noncompliance may result in internal employee complaints, external complaints filed with regulatory agencies, lawsuits with resultant payment of fines, damages, and costs, as well as the loss of qualified employees, and adverse media publicity.

Risk Assessment: High

Applicable Institution Policy:

Responsible Individual: EEO Officer or Human Resources Director

Specific Actions (Execution Control)	Evidence of Actions (Evidence of Control)	Review of Evidence (Supervisory Control)	Proof of Review (Evidence of Control)
Distribution of sexual harassment policy to all newly hired employees at New Employee Orientation (NEO).

Mandatory equal employment opportunity and sexual harassment training at NEO. | New employee signature on acknowledgement of receipt of sexual harassment training during NEO.

Training attendance sheets and agenda for NEO. | OHR review of training attendance sheets and agenda to assure that newly hired employees scheduled to attend NEO attended and that the orientation included the required sexual harassment training. | OHR reviewer's initials and date on review of training attendance sheets and agenda for NEO. |

The Institute of Internal Auditors Research Foundation

Specific Actions (Execution Control)	Evidence of Actions (Evidence of Control)	Review of Evidence (Supervisory Control)	Proof of Review (Evidence of Control)
Biennial onsite sexual harassment training for supervisors by the state Commission on Human Rights.	Training attendance sheets indicating training attended by supervisory employees.	OHR review of supervisory training attendance sheets to verify attendance of those scheduled to receive CHR training.	OHR reviewer's initials and date of review of supervisory training attendance sheets. OHR report of all supervisors scheduled, but not in attendance at the biennial sexual harassment training.
Intake, assessment, and investigation of all employee complaints that might be deemed to be sexual harassment.	Investigation report for each sexual harassment complaint.	OHR and/or EEO Office monitoring of sexual harassment complaints or preparation of formal report of findings concerning complaint.	OHR documentation of the disposition of all complaints involving sexual harassment, the action taken, and the appropriate OHR signature and date.
Periodic distribution of written sexual harassment policy with complaint procedures for sexual harassment and sexual misconduct to all employees.	Sexual harassment policy and signed acknowledgment form.	OHR placement of acknowledgment form into employee personnel file.	OHR report to compliance officer and supervisor of employees who have not completed sexual harassment training.

The Institute of Internal Auditors Research Foundation

APPENDIX J
SELF-ASSESSMENT INSTRUMENT

Purpose: To document the status of the Institutional Compliance Program after its initial implementation.

Source: All information has been obtained from institution staff through questionnaires, surveys, and interviews. Each working paper contains specific indications for the source of its information.

Objectives:

- To determine the implementation status of the *Action Plan to Ensure Institutional Compliance.*
- To verify the information reported to the System-wide Compliance Officer in the first year quarterly reports and the revised risk-based audit plan.
- To identify "best practices" in the program.
- To provide an external, objective assessment of the implementation of the institution compliance program
- To identify areas of needed improvement with recommendations for action, if appropriate.

	Question	Yes	No	W/P#	Status (Acceptable or NIP)	Related Recommendation
	INSTITUTIONAL COMPLIANCE COMMITTEE:					
1.	Does the Institutional Compliance Committee have a charter or other document detailing its duties and responsibilities? If yes, please provide copy.					

The Institute of Internal Auditors Research Foundation

Question	Yes	No	W/P#	Status (Acceptable or NIP)	Related Recommendation
2. Does the Compliance Committee consist of a cross-section of the Institution, including executive management, faculty, physicians, researchers, deans, department chairs, in addition to the high-risk areas? Provide list of members					
3. Has the Committee established a mechanism for the Compliance function, if a separate compliance function exists, to report its activity to the Committee? If yes, please provide copy					
4. Has the Committee established sub-committees to address each significant compliance area at the component? If yes, please provide sub-committee names, chairs, and members.					
5. Has the Committee established a mechanism to monitor activity in each "A" list risk area? If yes, please provide.					

The Institute of Internal Auditors Research Foundation

Question	Yes	No	W/P#	Status (Acceptable or NIP)	Related Recommendation
6. Does the Compliance Committee meet at least quarterly? Please provide minutes of each meeting					
7. Has the Committee performed a Self-Evaluation of its fiscal year 1999 activities? If yes, please provide.					
8. Has the Committee performed an evaluation of the Compliance Officer's performance in fiscal 1999? If yes, please provide.					
9. Does the Committee have a mechanism for determining that appropriate corrective, restorative, and/or disciplinary action has been taken for each event of noncompliance? If yes, please provide.					

Question	Yes	No	W/P#	Status (Acceptable or NIP)	Related Recommendation
COMPLIANCE OFFICER AND FUNCTION					
10. Is the Compliance Officer a high-ranking administrative officer at the component who has direct access to the Chief Administrative Officer?					

11. Has the component provided sufficient resources for the Compliance Officer to adequately carry out those functions defined in the Action Plan that are applicable to the component?
  Budget?
  Staff?
  Sub-committees?
Please provide organization chart and/or budget					

12. Do the Compliance Officer and each employee in the Compliance function have a job description? If yes, please provide.					
13. Does the Compliance function provide oversight controls for the high-risk areas? If yes, please describe the oversight controls performed for each applicable high-risk area. Include oversight inspection programs and the results of performing those programs.					

Question	Yes	No	W/P#	Status (Acceptable or NIP)	Related Recommendation
14. Have Compliance function staff received external training related to operating an institutional compliance program? Provide information on all such training, including content, presenter, and attendees.					
15. Does the Compliance Officer provide regular updates on Compliance activities to the Chief Administrative Officer? If yes, describe how and how often.					
16. Does the Compliance Officer file all required reports in a timely fashion? Confidential Reporting Mechanism Activity Quarterly Activity Report Annual Risk-Based Compliance Plan					
17. Has the Compliance Officer ensured that all employees have received General Compliance Training? If yes, provide the training records. If no, have any employees received this training?					
18. If General Compliance Training has not been provided to all employees, is there a detailed plan to accomplish that? If yes, please provide the plan.					

Question	Yes	No	W/P#	Status (Acceptable or NIP)	Related Recommendation
19. Has the Compliance Officer established a Confidential Reporting Mechanism? If yes, please provide a description and a summary of all activity to date, including the number of reports received to date.					
20. Has the Compliance Officer developed a compliance manual? If yes, please provide.					
RISK ASSESSMENT PROCESS					
21. Has a detailed inventory of all compliance issues applicable to the component been performed? Federal? State? Local? Regulators/Accreditors? UT System? Component? If yes, please provide.					
22. Was the inventory performed by Sub-committees? Functional Departments? Management?					

Question	Yes	No	W/P#	Status (Acceptable or NIP)	Related Recommendation
23. Were all risks included, even those that the component believes are adequately controlled? If no, provide a list of those risk not included in the inventory for any reason					
24. Has the probability of occurrence and the potential impact been estimated for each risk listed? If yes, provide the methodology for assigning these values.					
25. Has the inventory of risks been ranked from most critical to least critical? If yes, provide methodology for determining the rankings.					
26. Has a methodology been established for determining High-risk or "A" list items. Please provide the methodology and the resultant "A" list					
EACH "A" LIST RISK (Please provide details when answers are "yes")					
27. Has a single responsible person been designated?					
28. Has a monitoring plan been developed for the risk?					

Question	Yes	No	W/P#	Status (Acceptable or NIP)	Related Recommendation
29. Does the monitoring plan describe what operating controls will be monitored?					
30. Does the monitoring plan detail the actions to be taken to determine whether or not the operating controls were applied correctly?					
31. Is there documented evidence that the monitoring controls were performed?					
32. Is there documented evidence of the results of the monitoring controls?					
33. Is there documented evidence of actions taken when monitoring controls identify failure of operating controls?					
34. Are instances of noncompliance documented and dealt with appropriately?					
35. Are instances of noncompliance or potential noncompliance reported to the Compliance Committee and to the Chief Administrative Officer?					
36. Has documented specialized training relative to mitigation of this risk been provided to all employees who interact with the risk?					

Question	Yes	No	W/P#	Status (Acceptable or NIP)	Related Recommendation
37. Has documented specialized training been provided in each case of failure of operating controls or instances of noncompliance?					
38. Does the high-risk area responsible person provide quarterly and other reports of all activities to the Compliance Officer and the Compliance Committee?					
INTERNAL AUDITING					
39. Has an initial audit been performed of the design of the component's institutional compliance program?					
40. Has a follow-up to the initial audit been performed?					
41. Has the internal audit department performed design audits of any high-risk area monitoring plans?					
42. Has the internal audit department performed a design audit of any Compliance function oversight controls?					
43. Has internal audit performed any other types of audits involving compliance risks?					

The Institute of Internal Auditors Research Foundation

APPENDIX K
GLOSSARY

"A" Risks	Uncertainties that, if realized, would have a significant impact on the achievement of goals and objectives, specifically compliance goals and objectives.
Agreed-upon Procedures	An assurance strategy in which the compliance officer contracts with the internal auditing function to perform specified information gathering procedures on high risk areas for the compliance officer.
Assurance Strategy	A process used by one party to add value to information that is to be used by another party.
"B" Risks	Uncertainties that, if realized, would not have a significant impact on the achievement of goals and objectives, specifically compliance goals and objectives.
Certification	An assurance strategy in which the reporting manager adds value to the information that the manager reports to the compliance officer by signing a statement that the information is factual.
Chief Administrative Officer	See Chief Executive Officer.
Chief Executive Officer	The highest-ranking operational officer at an institution.
Compliance Committee	The group of executive managers appointed by the chief executive officer to provide guidance, and advice to the compliance office in establishing and operating the compliance program.
Compliance Committee Working Group	The group of risk area managers appointed by the compliance committee with advice from the compliance officer to advise and assist in the performance of specific tasks in the compliance program, such as developing a risk-based plan, ensuring awareness, and evaluating reports from the "A" risk responsible parties.

The Institute of Internal Auditors Research Foundation

Compliance Coordinator	The person appointed by the compliance officer to manage the day-to-day operations of the compliance program, regardless of the specific title held, such as director, executive director, assistant compliance officer, or coordinator.
Compliance Function	Those employees of the institution that provide support services for the compliance officer either as direct employees or through agreements with other functions in the institution.
Compliance Officer	The senior management representative of the chief executive officer who is responsible for the establishment of a compliance infrastructure.
Compliance Program	The formal effort of the institution, sanctioned by the governance function, to minimize instances of noncompliance through a permanent infrastructure that includes training, monitoring, and reporting.
Confidential Reporting Mechanism	Any process whereby employees can report suspected instances of noncompliance to institution management anonymously and without fear of reprisal.
Consequences of Noncompliance	The actions that have been prescribed and will be taken by management when instances of noncompliance are identified.
COSO	The internal control model used in the U.S.
Design Audit	An assurance strategy performed by internal auditing to provide information to the governance function and executive management that a program's design meets an established set of criteria; it does not include assurance about the operation of the program.

The Institute of Internal Auditors Research Foundation

Execution Controls	Those procedures that are applied by operating staff to every event/transaction in a process at the time of its creation to ensure compliance with the policies and procedures governing the process.
Executive Management	The senior managers of the institution who report directly to the chief executive officer.
Exposure	The total amount of physical, financial, human, information, or reputation assets subject to a particular risk.
False Claims Act	A federal law dealing with false claims for funds filed with a United States government entity or program.
Federal Sentencing Guidelines	Federal law pertaining to the assessment of damages in cases of fraud against the United States government, its agencies and departments, and the programs it funds.
General Compliance Training	Training made available to all institution employees to: (1) make them aware of their responsibilities for compliance and ethics, (2) inform them of basic compliance issues applicable to all employees, (3) provide them with information on where to get specific questions answered, and (4) inform them on how to anonymously report noncompliance.
General Compliance Training Plan	The document that specifies the general compliance training program content, delivery mechanisms, delivery schedule, and reporting activities for the current and subsequent year.
Governance Function	The policy-setting body of the institution, usually a board of regents or board of governors.
Information Validation Audit	An assurance strategy performed by internal auditing to provide information to the governance function and executive management on whether or not a program's operations conform to the program's design.

The Institute of Internal Auditors Research Foundation

Inspection	An assurance strategy performed by the compliance function to validate the information provided to the compliance officer by an "A" risk responsible party.
Instances of Noncompliance	Documented events or transactions that do not conform to the applicable laws, rules, and regulations, and policies and procedures.
Institutional Compliance Program	See Compliance Program.
Internal Auditing	A function (department) that provides assurance services and consulting services for the governance function and management.
Monitoring Controls	See Supervisory Controls.
Monitoring Plan	The definition of (1) execution controls that must be performed as designed to minimize instances of noncompliance, (2) appropriate documentation of the execution controls application, (3) supervisory controls that will be used to ensure execution controls are applied as designed, and (4) appropriate documentation of the supervisory controls application.
Operating Controls	See Execution Controls.
Other External Assurance Providers	Government auditors, accreditation organizations, regulators, public accounting firms, trade organizations, and other recognized groups that independently assess the design of activities and the validity of information produced by activities.
Oversight Controls	Those procedures applied by middle and senior management soon after an event/transaction has occurred to ensure that supervisory controls have been applied as designed, including review of status reports, exception reports, actual v. planned analysis, etc.

PATH Audit	Federal government audit of billing activities of physicians at teaching hospitals.
Peer Review	An organized study of an operation, program, process, or function conducted by persons from outside the studied area who are "experts" in the subject being studied.
Predefined Set of Consequences of Noncompliance	The sanctions specified in the policies and procedures of a process that will be taken by management when it is factually determined that an employee has failed to comply with the laws, rules, and regulations, and policies and procedures prescribed by the process.
Reporting Plan	The definition of what the responsible party will report to the compliance officer and when it will be reported.
Responsible Party	The one employee (management, faculty, or staff) who is responsible for the management of a particular compliance risk or risk area.
Risk Area	A homogeneous activity (can be a process, department, function) in which there are compliance risks; examples, student financial aid, intercollegiate athletics, research, instruction, fiscal management, environmental health and safety, human resources, etc.
Risk Assessment	The identification, measurement, and prioritization of the compliance risks of the work unit, risk area, or institution.
Risks	Uncertainties that can impact the ability of the institution to achieve its goals and objectives; specifically, its goals and objectives to comply with all laws, rules, and regulations, and policies and procedures which govern its operations.
Specialized Training	Training in the understanding and application of laws, rules and regulations, and policies and procedures that apply to operations in a specific risk area.

Specialized Training Plan	The definition of who will receive specialized training applicable to a risk area, the content of the training, and the frequency of the training.
Standards of Conduct Guide	A compilation of basic information on those already existing laws, rules, and regulations, and policies and procedures governing the operations of the institution that apply to employees generally, including information on where to find out more information about each issue.
Subject Matter Experts	Individuals who are known to have a greater than average knowledge of the laws, rules, and regulations, and policies and procedures that are applicable to a specific risk area.
Supervisory Controls	Those procedures performed at the origination of an event/transaction or immediately thereafter by first line management (or a representative of first line management) on a sample of all events/transactions to determine that the execution controls have been applied as designed.
Work Unit	The organizational level of the institution at which events/transactions are originated.

The Institute of Internal Auditors Research Foundation

APPENDIX L
ASSURANCE CONTINUUM MODEL
FOR THE 21ST CENTURY

Collaborative Assurance
(Governance and Management Control Processes)

I----------I   ←Periodic Assurance→   I----------I
(Governance Control Processes)

I----------Ongoing Assurance----------I
(Management Control Processes)

Internal Audit Controls	Execution Controls	Supervisory Controls	Oversight Controls	Internal Audit Controls
Pre-operations design review of ongoing assurance	During execution of event or transaction	Immediately after execution of event or transaction	Soon after execution of event or transaction	Post-operations audit of execution of ongoing assurance

Note: The Assurance Continuum, developed by David Crawford, is an enhancement to the Levels of Control in the COSO Model authored by Crawford and published in the October 2000 issue of *Internal Auditor*. The information on pages 188 through 190 of Appendix L is from that article and is included here to explain the levels of control in the Assurance Continuum. Portions of the article were reprinted with permission from the October 2000 issue of *Internal Auditor*, published by The Insitute of Internal Auditors, Inc.

The Institute of Internal Auditors Research Foundation

Execution Controls
(Operating Controls)

- Embedded in day-to-day operations
  - Policies and procedures
  - Segregation of duties
  - Reconciliations/comparisons
- Performed on every event/transaction
- Performed by the generators of the event/transaction
- Performed in "real time," as the event/transaction is executed

---

Supervisory Controls
(Monitoring Controls)

- Reapplication of operating controls
  - Supervisory Review; Quality Assurance; Self-assessment
- Performed very soon after the generation of the event/transaction
- Performed by line management or staff positions who do not originate the event/transaction
- Performed on a sample of the total number of events/transactions

---

**Oversight Controls
(Executive Controls)**

- Exception reports, status reports, analytical reviews, variance analysis
- Performed by representatives of executive management
- Performed on information provided by supervisory management
- Performed within a short period (weeks/months) after the event/transaction is originated

---

**Internal Audit Controls
(Governance Controls)**

- Audit of the design of controls, not the operation of controls
- Performed either before the event/transaction is originated or long after
- Performed by staff with no involvement in the operations
- Performed on individual events/transactions for discovery only

---

Collaborative Assurance Model				
Level of Assurance Provided	Execution Controls Performed by	Supervisory Controls Performed by	Oversight Controls Performed by	I/A Controls Performed by
Optimal	Management	Management	Management	Internal Audit
Acceptable	Management	Management	Internal Audit	Internal Audit
Marginal	Management	Internal Audit	Internal Audit	Internal Audit
Unacceptable	Internal Audit	Internal Audit	Internal Audit	Internal Audit
Unacceptable	Management	Management	Management	Management

The Institute of Internal Auditors Research Foundation

IIA Research Foundation
Board of Research Advisors
2001/2002

The Institute of Internal Auditors Research Foundation

IIA RESEARCH FOUNDATION

Chairman's Circle

AT&T
Cargill, Inc.
General Motors Corporation
Microsoft Corporation
PepsiCo, Inc.
PricewaterhouseCoopers LLP

The Institute of Internal Auditors Research Foundation